Table of Contents

Note

INTRODUCTION

CHAPTER ONE

Why this may be the most important purchasing book you will ever read.

Contracts are commonplace for a person who is involved in the field of purchasing. Most days are spent negotiating contracts, forming contracts or executing contracts that have already been formed. However, it is not just people in Purchasing or business people who deal with contracts on a daily basis. In fact, every person in our society enters into contracts dozens of times every day. Every time we enter into a business deal, use a credit card or even buy an item at a store, we enter into a contract.

Most of these contracts are never reduced to writing. And for the most part, enforcing these agreements is never a problem. They are one time happenings where both sides perform simultaneously. Because of that, there is no need to reduce the transaction to writing. If contracts do need to be written down, they can be as simple as writing a few items down on a napkin and signing it. A majority of contracts don't even have to be in writing. You pick out a piece of computer equipment, pay for it and take it back to the office. You have entered into a contract and are given a receipt to show as evidence. Because contracts are so common in our society, most people overlook them...until something goes wrong.

What exactly did you buy when you bought that computer? In fact, you actually entered into more contracts then you may think. What about the software that was on the computer? Did you buy the software that was on the computer, or did you also enter into several software licensing agreements? Do you have the right to return that computer or have it fixed if it doesn't work when you open the box? The answers may be governed by the contract you entered into with the manufacturer of the computer. Or, they may be governed by the contract you entered into with the company that sold you the computer. Maybe you also used a company credit card to pay for the computer. In that case, you entered into an additional contract with the credit card company. You can now see you entered into two or three contracts when you bought the computer and were not even aware of that fact. If you didn't know you entered into a contract, how can you know what is in the contract?

How many people have signed a contract without ever reading what was in it?

People leave it up to lawyers to draft an agreement and then are afraid to ask when they do not understand the terms or concepts of the contract. Of course, it is hard to have problems with a contract when you don't even read it. A person received a contract from a lawyer and gives it to his lawyer, never looking at it himself. People leave it to their lawyers and complain when they are not happy. As the person entering into the contract, it is your responsibility to read what you are signing and make sure you can live with those terms.

Most people blame lawyers for the problems of society. How about the old joke: Why don't sharks eat lawyers?

Professional Courtesy.

Lawyers are not the problem, clients are. A lawyer may be nasty, but it is most likely because the client is telling him to do that. Remember, lawyers work for clients and are bound by ethical principles to do what is in the best interests of their clients. The problems arise when lawyers and their clients do not communicate. If lawyers are not told otherwise, they are going to do what they believe is in the best interest of their clients, not what is fair and not what is nice. A lawyer can only do what a client tells him, and even that can become increasingly difficult when a client is always changing his mind about what he wants or when he does not even bother to look at what the lawyer is doing.

When it comes to contracts, every lawyer has his or her own way of doing things, and every lawyer has a way he likes to draft contracts. That does not mean that any one way is right. Contract clauses can be as simple or as complex as people want. It depends on how airtight the clauses need to be. In the end, it all comes down to whether or not the contract is enforceable. Anything can be put into a contract. What the courts of the United States will and will not uphold is a different story. That is why lawyers are important. They are best prepared to tell you what should or should not be in your contract.

It is up to the people to be clear about what they want, and then to communicate that to the people writing the contracts. I am a lawyer, and my job is writing contracts. When I first started I was amazed at how difficult it was to put what you wanted into writing. Contracts are supposed to be simple, but we have made them very complex documents. That is because we, as a society, have become lawsuit happy. When something goes wrong we do not try to work it out with the other side; we just sue them. We spend, in some cases, tens of thousands of dollars to litigate over matters that could have been settled with a simple phone call and a few kind words. We sue, even though, in many cases, you can be awarded hundreds of thousands of dollars and never collect a penny.

Relationships that at one time, were based on mutual trust, are now adversarial. We want to make the offending party pay for what he/she did wrong. We tell our lawyers "Go get them," forgetting about the reason we entered into the contract in the first place. People forget that, for the most part, contracts are living documents, especially in the field of purchasing. That means the contract we enter into today will likely be in effect for years. Consequently, there will always be a need to talk to and cooperate with the other side. You must be prepared for all contingencies. A tightly drawn contract will prevent the other party from doing things that should hopefully, prevent you from having to go to court to try to collect monies for the other side's wrongdoings.

Stages of a Contract

Although I will talk about negotiations in this book only briefly, they may be just as important as the actual writing of the contract. I tell my clients that the negotiation process is ongoing, even after the contract is written and signed. You must realize that since you'll be dealing with the other side after you sign the contract, you need to have a win/win outcome at the negotiation, execution and performance stages.

The negotiation stage takes place up to the point when the contract is drafted. This topic is covered in general negotiation books. Ideally, you would like a win/win negotiation where both sides are happy with the outcome and then are able to proceed to the execution stage. It is difficult to get to the execution stage if you cannot deal with the negotiation process. In the field of purchasing, you need to walk a thin line between getting the best deal for your company and making sure that the other side is also happy with the deal's outcome.

Until a contract is signed there is no agreement. For the most part, every single clause in a contract will be agreed upon separately. You will need to know what they mean, as well as being aware of clauses that you want in contracts which may not be in the document at the start.

The execution stage takes place when the contract is drafted and signed. You are still negotiating at this stage but, for the most part, you are debating what clauses should and should not be in the agreement and what the language of those clauses should be. This stage is the focus of this book. Although I do deal with all three stages, this book primarily focuses on what to do after negotiations and how to draft a contract that you can live with today and tomorrow.

The final stage is the performance stage. Contrary to popular belief, you are still negotiating even after you enter into the contract. You may suddenly need more or less of a product. You may want to pay a little late. Your end product might go through a change and you might not need the product from your supplier anymore. All of this requires that the existing contract be modified, or in some cases canceled. The point is the contract must address anything that can potentially happen after the agreement is executed. Because of those potential problems and pitfalls, this book also deals with what can go wrong, how to prepare yourself for the worst and how to plan for those contingencies when you draft your contract.

I am continually amazed that people spend so much time negotiating a few contract terms like price and delivery schedule and spend so little time on the rest of the contract, especially when in the overall purchasing process so little time is spent in actually drafting the contract and agreeing on what clauses will be included. I see companies spending two years working on a Request for Proposal, getting bids and choosing a supplier. Then they draft the contract they are entering into which will, in some cases, govern their relationship with the other side for the next few years and that contract contains a limitation of liability clause or a mutual termination for convenience clause.

You also have to address the issue of which party's contract you will start with, who will write it and what you will do if something goes wrong. Law students spend a good portion of their first year in law school learning about contracts. For the most part, the average person knows only what they are told by lawyers, usually learning only when something goes wrong.

Many people pull an old contract out of a drawer and use it years later when they need a new one, unaware that laws may have changed and the contract they used one or two years ago may no longer meet their needs, or, they get a contract in the mail from the other side and simply sign it, never even considering the possibility of negotiating the terms.

This book is intended to introduce you to contracts, what should be in them and what clauses in the contract can look like. All a contract has to do is follow a few basic requirements to be enforceable. Everything else is up to you.

But be warned. This book is not intended to be a bible. There is no way that a book this size could ever tell you everything you are going to need to know about contracts and purchasing. No book ever could. I have found that experience, and in most cases making mistakes are the best teachers.

Do not copy what is in this book, use it and then be surprised when you don't like the outcome. This book is meant to make you think about what you want. A contract does not have to be in legal mumbo jumbo with a lot of big words. The bottom line is to write it so that you understand what is going on. I use a simple rule. Give the contract to a person who knows nothing about what you are doing. If they can read the contract and tell you all about what is happening, you're doing well.

This book was originally intended to be part of a series of books on various purchasing topics. It is my belief that this was the most important part of that series, because everything else you do is only worth what is written in the contract. It doesn't matter how carefully you prepared your Request for Proposal, how many bids you received, or how well you negotiated your deal, if you can't live with the contract in five years or if someone does something wrong and you can't do anything about it.

Remember that you are working together at the time you enter into the contract. While everything may be fine now, that can all change in a second. One missed shipment, one defective part, or one employee leaving can spell trouble if a contract is not carefully drafted. How many of you have been told, "You don't have to put that in the contact, I'll do it?" How many of you believed it and were surprised when it didn't happen? You have to decide what you are going to do if anything goes wrong. You must prepare for every contingency.

Contracts also have to deal with what you want to protect. Maybe you are entering into a close relationship with the other side and will be revealing many company secrets. Maybe your employees are going to be working at another company for a long period of time. Maybe your employees will need considerable training, and you plan to spend a great deal of money on this training. You might suddenly have to work with third party suppliers or buy new pieces of equipment. If you think you might face any of these situations you will find that you may be entering into two or more additional contracts than the one you were originally negotiating.

You may also need to consider drafting contracts with a third party supplier, employees or other outside parties. Remember to carefully consider every angle of your situation. This is a big topic, and a book this size can only scratch the surface. What it can do for you is inform you and give you knowledge that can help you immensely.

When I teach negotiations I constantly talk about power. It is the most important aspect of negotiations. If you cannot be powerful, you cannot get what you want. Every contract term is one more thing that must be negotiated. I advise that before you even go into contract negotiations you have a contract written. I go into some negotiations with a contract already loaded onto my laptop computer. As we talk, I edit the contract, and when the negotiations are settled, we sign the contract right away. Remember that knowledge is power, and any leverage you have will help you get the most out of your contracts.

You also have to be aware of the fact that even if a contract is missing items there are laws that may fill in those terms. Laws permeate our society, but these laws vary from state to state. What is allowed in some places may not be allowed in others. Federal rules and regulations may govern what can and cannot be in your contract. Or, you may find that you have no choice at all about what is in your contract.

For example, if you are dealing with the government, you have little, if any say in what is going to be in your agreement. Either you sign the agreement or you don't. That is all well and good, but that does not mean that you should not read the contract. I hear it all the time from people: I had to sign the contract so it didn't matter what was in it. That is not true. If you are going to sign the contract, at least read it so you know what is required of you.

Hopefully, this book will empower you with the ability to carefully review any contract, whether it be Purchasing related or not. It should give you the insight to know what you can and cannot live with. You should also come away with a "wish list" of those things that, ideally, you want in any contract you sign.

One final note, contracts are complex, legal, documents. They are not books. Read your contracts actively, pen in hand. Take notes and write down questions. Remember, it is hard to enforce a provision you don't know anything about. Even to this day, I am still learning and growing in my knowledge of contracts. Go take a class. Join an organization. Become powerful.

Best of luck, and happy contracting.

THE BASICS OF PURCHASING LAW

CHAPTER TWO

As a power purchasing professional you do not want to have to worry about all of the ins and outs of contracts. However, everyone must understand that contracts are a part of everyday life. People in the field of purchasing, more than almost everyone else, see contracts on a daily basis and form agreements constantly. For the purchasing professional, contracts permeate every part of your day-to-day business dealings.

The strangest part of being in Purchasing has to be the fact that when you start with your company everything is usually already in place. You are not asked to draft contracts and reinvent the wheel. More likely than not, your company has been in business for some time and probably has a standard way of doing things. You are simply asked to keep doing things the same way.

Far too often we are reduced to standard form contracts. The purchase order you use in your business has been used for the last 20 years. Why, because it has always been done that way. Well, times change, and contracts need to change along with them. You will hear me tell you over and over again in this book that contracts are living documents. Signing a contact does not mean it is written in stone and cannot be changed.

Things happen, and as a result, your contract needs to be flexible enough to take those things into account. For example, your customer of the last ten years wants to change the destination of the goods you send him from Ohio to California. The contract states quite clearly that the goods are to go to Ohio. Do you say "no"? Of course not, you will change the contract to meet the new needs of your customer.

For basically the same reasons, the boiler plate of your contract needs to change as well. Laws can change significantly over time. You need to be aware of these variations and changes and to take them into account in your agreement.

There are several objectives that you should achieve in reading this book. First and foremost, I hope to increase your awareness regarding contracts. The better informed you are the better you will be able to use contracts to meet your needs. Consider everything I teach you to be a tool. The more tools you have the better you can do your job.

Later in the book I provide many standard clauses for contracts so you can review them and know you have choices about the contracts. Knowledge is power. Knowing these clauses will help you to develop skills and to use those skills in drafting agreements. You will also be able to understand the meaning of each of the clauses you have.

How many of us sign contracts without reading them? I'm a lawyer, and I have done it. When I purchased my house, I signed the documents then went home and kicked myself for not taking the time to read the 30+ pages I had been given. My thinking at the time was typical of most people: I thought I would not be able to change anything in the contract so why take the time to read it.

But, that's not the point. I didn't need to read the contract because I wanted to change it. I needed to read the contract because I was signing my name to it and was going to commit myself to a series of promises. It was important for me to know exactly what those promises were and exactly what was expected of me.

When I first started practicing law, I had a client who signed a lease for a building to house her business. Before the signing, I reviewed the lease, suggested some changes that would protect her and negotiated for those changes. The two parties signed the contract, and my client leased the property. For the first year there were no problems.

The contract contained a provision to increase the rent at the end of the year based upon an increase in the cost of living. My client came to me at the start of the second year when her landlord wanted to increase her rent based on the provision. I assumed my client had read the contract and knew exactly what to expect. In fact, I never discussed price with the landlord on my client's behalf. I had assumed that this was all agreed upon.

My client had not included this issue in the list of problems she had with the lease.

My mistake was in not making sure my client knew every clause of the contract she was entering into. Her mistake was in leaving everything to a lawyer who could never know all the aspects of what she did and did not agree to. I handle clients very differently now. No matter how long the contract is, I go through it page by page with my clients making sure they understand each and every provision. Of course, time is money, and I have to charge for the extra time these discussions take. But time and time again I see people sign contracts they don't read. Let me assure you that it is the biggest mistake people make.

It is even more important that as purchasing professionals you examine and consistently review your agreements. Purchasing people are among the busiest in corporate life. There is not a lot of time available. It is easy not to take the time to review your agreements, but it must be done. It is your job.

In my first job we developed a policy and procedure manual for purchasing professionals to follow. These were standard guidelines about what they could and could not do. For example, the spending limits for buyers' purchases were clearly spelled out. Among the requirements for every person were the guidelines for continuing education. We wanted everyone to be well educated in the field of contracts. You need to review what your company requires of you regarding contracts. First, ask if you even have the authority to enter into a contract. If you do, what does your company require to be included in the contract?

What is a Contract?

Basically, purchasing is acquiring a good or service for money or other consideration. And every time you purchase something you enter into a contract. In general, most purchasing professionals use purchase orders as a way of contracting for the goods and services they need.

However, purchase orders are minimal contracts at best. They are orders for goods or services, which list some of the basics that you want. For example, the terms, price, place of delivery, and quantities for specific items may all be on the purchase order. But many things, such as governing law, may not be on the purchase order. There is also the other extreme. I saw a purchase order from a client who tried to fit so much into the purchase order that the type ended up so small you could not read it. I also see people not even providing terms and conditions at all, simply referencing a web site on the front of their purchase order. People cannot be bound to terms and conditions they have never been given.

So then, what is a contract? In short, a contract is a promise the law will enforce. Pretty easy, right? But, think of all of the grey areas in this definition. How do we know what kind of agreements the law will enforce unless we go to court and have a court rubber stamp the agreement as enforceable? Of course, we don't want to have to check with the court every time we have an agreement. Contracts can be very beneficial for us, Supplier Certification, ISO standards, Activity Based Costing and similar topics permeate business life today. Why? Each of the current "hot" topics comes up because of contracts. Businesses want to look at how suppliers are performing. They want to enter into long-term contracts with suppliers based upon a reduction of material costs and reliable standards of quality. These are going to be essential elements of the contracts into which businesses will enter.

One of the basic tenants of society is that every person has the freedom to enter into contracts. We do not want the government, or anyone else for that matter, telling us that we cannot do things. We want to decide for ourselves. However, we also want certainty. We want to know the contracts we enter into are enforceable and rely on those contracts since they affect our behavior.

So, what exactly do we want? Well, we want to have some type of standards that tell us what kind of agreements we can and cannot enter into. We also want to know what consequences our actions will have.

The Uniform Commercial Code (UCC) is a set of laws, which

guides people who enter into commercial transactions. The UCC, adopted by every state applies to sales of goods. The UCC defines goods as all things, which are movable at the time they are identified to the contract. It was designed to give guidance to business people in their dealings but can be modified by the provisions in a contract. The UCC does not apply to services, leases or construction agreements.

If a contract deals with both goods and services it is important to determine which element of the contract is dominant. If goods dominate, the UCC applies. If services dominate, common law will apply. Common law consists of the decisions handed down by judges in the various cases that come before them. These decisions are collected in books, which lawyers refer to in an effort to guide how they advise their clients.

UCC's Article 2 specifically governs the sale of goods. Other articles of the UCC cover various other commercial transactions such as banking (Article 4), warehouse transactions (Article 7), bulk transfers (Article 6) and commercial paper (Article 3).

Contracts can be expressed or implied, formal or informal, oral or written, long or short. But no matter what form a contract takes the same basics apply. Most contracts are bilateral which means that two people are making promises. They can also be unilateral where only one party makes a promise which is subject to enforceability.

The basic problem with all contracts is determining their enforceability. We can look to several places to give us guidance about what types of items are enforceable. Contract law give lawyers a body of rulings by the courts about what has and has not worked in the past. Also formal laws such as the Uniform Commercial Code give the actual laws that must be followed by all of us and guide our conduct.

The objective is to meet the reasonable expectations of the parties. What did everyone want when they signed this agreement? What did everyone believe they were agreeing to?

An agreement can be as simple as someone writing on a piece

of paper "I will sell you my car for $10", and the parties signing the paper.
Or it can be as formal as a 100 page document with numerous attachments.
They both accomplish the exact same thing: they tell you what the parties
intended to do. The important thing is whether or not all elements of a
contract exist and whether or not the agreement will be enforceable by the
courts.

Often times you will see the words contract and agreement in
this book. They are not the same thing. An agreement is much broader
than a contract. You and I can enter into negotiations and reach an
agreement. That does not mean we have a contract. A contract comes from
an agreement, which is enforceable by courts. We will talk about all the
elements of a contract. However, we can assume, for the purposes of this
book, that when two parties enter into an agreement they intend there to
be a contact.

Of course you will never get to the elements of a contract if
there is no agreement as to what the elements of the contract will be. That
is why negotiations are so important.

THE ROLE OF NEGOTIATIONS IN CONTRACT LAW

CHAPTER THREE

Oddly enough, this may be the most important chapter of the book, and it has very little to do with the actual contract that parties will enter into. Every contract requires a negotiation. And negotiations are ongoing, even after entering into the contract. Remember, contracts are living documents.

Just as I have recommended you take the time to learn about contracts, you must also take the time to learn how to negotiate. The goal in most negotiations is win/win. We want both sides to feel like they are getting something positive out of the negotiations. Win/win outcomes should be the goal of every negotiation. This means that not only do you want a favorable outcome for yourself but for the other side as well. If you want a win/win outcome you need to have high trust and high cooperation between both sides. Trust and cooperation serve as the foundation upon which we build win/win outcomes. On that foundation you will build a house, which represents the agreement reached between the parties. The stronger the trust and cooperation, the stronger the house, and the better the chance your agreement will stand the test of time.

I'm amazed how lazy a society we have become. In the past people seemed to want to negotiate. I make fun of a friend of mine because he negotiates everything. He goes to the supermarket and finds a bruised piece of fruit and offers less than the price marked. He goes to dinner and complains about the food and negotiates free desert. For him, the fun is in the effort, not the outcome.

Today, we don't want to negotiate at all. Most of us don't like the stress of trying to agree on a price. Society and marketing professionals would have us believe that things are not negotiable at all. A perfect example of these elements has occurred in the auto industry. Everyone used to know that when it came to buying a car you went to the dealer and negotiated the best price you could get. The sales person said he would have to go check with his manager and then would disappear into the back somewhere.

You would wait at the salesman's desk, and he would return several minutes later and tell you what the manager said. You would never meet this "manager". But, when you left you would feel like you negotiated for the best price and that you got a great deal for the car. Today, many car dealers make a point of advertising, "no hassle buying", playing up their policy of no negotiation pricing. The price on the sticker is the price of the car; you either pay it or don't buy the car.

Strangely enough, people seem to love this new process. There was such a distrust of sales people in the auto industry that we would rather not deal with them. We would prefer not to negotiate. However, negotiations are vital to the purchasing professional.

Most negotiations can be classified as a ritual. For example, you want to buy one pound of oranges at the local outdoor market. The price is $5. You offer less than the posted price, say $4, but you don't really care because you are not trying to build a long term relationship with anyone. All you care about is saving money on this one purchase. You dicker with the sales person and end up splitting the difference and spending $4.50. This is not a win/win negotiation because you have not built the trust that forms part of the requirements of a win/win outcome.

But, let's say that instead of buying one pound of oranges you want to buy 1000 pounds. Of course you can no longer look at all of the oranges to ensure their quality. You must trust the sales person. Also, you know you don't want to pay the same five dollars the supplier offered for a single pound. You are not even willing to pay the $4.50 you had agreed to previously. Instead, you want a negotiation that will form the basis of a partnership. You are going to want a win/win outcome.

There will have to be careful negotiations to reach an agreement, which benefit both parties. Other things need consideration as well: date, time and place of delivery, for example. These were not considerations when only one pound of oranges was to be purchased. Now, however, you might be willing to trade some dollars to get favorable delivery conditions.

Stages of Negotiations

Stage One

How do you prepare for this type of negotiation, and what is needed to succeed?

First, you must decide what your opening position will be. You do not want to open up with a position that is so unreasonable that you are going to hurt the bargaining process. However, you also do not want to seem like a pushover. This is going to take research into factors like:

- Typical Cost

- Type and Size

- Quality of the Supplier

- Other factors that you consider important

You can use each of these items to influence what you will do in the negotiation process.

For example, if you discover the orange growing region and your supplier experienced an unusually bad frost this year and more than half of the oranges were destroyed, you will be prepared to pay more for oranges. Also, due to this, you may consider postponing entering into the contract. You do not want to enter into a long- term supply agreement this year. Since you know prices are going to be higher than average this year, you don't want to use this year to set a base line for the prices you are going to pay in the future.

You will also determine what type of negotiation style you will use. Just as an actor assumes a role in a play, you will assume a role in your dealings with the other side. You will need to stick to that role as well, so you want to choose a negotiation style that will fit with your character. For example, when my partner and I negotiate we often assume the styles of good guy/bad guy: one of us is the tough negotiator and the other, the easy going friend.

This style is often effective in very tough negotiations where any concession will be hard to get from the other side. You want to make it look like everything you give up is vitally important and a lot of work. This way they will think twice before asking concessions of you. It is also easier to get concessions from the other side because they are willing to give things up to make you happy.

All negotiations are about power. He who has the most power controls the negotiation and thus, achieves the more favorable outcome. Power can be given, and power can be taken away. For example, if you change your style of negotiation you will lose power. If my partner and I start off as good guy and bad guy and then we both become pushovers, obviously, the other side will no longer take us seriously. As a result, our ability to get a favorable outcome will be impaired.

Just as we may have different negotiating styles, different cultures negotiate differently. The Japanese style uses the team approach to negotiations: they send in a group of people and constantly change whom you talk to. The Russian style attempts to bully you with their position and assumes a "take it or leave it" attitude without room for negotiation.

To determine the most effective style, you must decide what outcome you want and then pick a style that fits. If you want a win/win outcome, for example, you will have to pick a style that builds upon the foundations of partnership and trust. You want the partnership to carry over from the negotiation to the performance of the contract you are entering into.

In the previous example, where the car salesman disappears into the back to talk with his "manager", we see another effective negotiation technique. Whether or not you ever see the manager you should realize that you are not dealing with the right person; you are not negotiating with the person who has the authority to enter into the deal you are making. Remember: never deal with the monkey when you should be dealing with the organ grinder.

The manager never comes out to talk to you because it is easier to turn you down. You sit and you wait. Every time you offer something else you know you have to spend more time waiting. Soon, you start thinking: It's my favorite car, and I want it now. You get tired of waiting, so you give up. The fact that the manager is not there with you gives the other side more power over you and influence over the outcome of the negotiation. Remember, this is not a win/win situation. What I recommend is simple: before you begin negotiations, be sure you are talking to the right person.

You need to talk to someone who has the ability to make the agreement that you want. Notice I said the agreement that you want. This implies that you know what you want. Once you determine what you want, check with the other side and find out the position of the person they are sending. Also, be wary of conference calls. I always like to see the other side face to face. Depending on the amount of money you are talking about it may be worth the plane ride.

I had a client who negotiated a multi-million dollar deal. We had eight or nine negotiation sessions with the other side, who drafted the contract. For over three months I never met them face-to-face. All the phone conversations with them were very rushed. They always had to go to a meeting. They would frequently revisit issues we had previously agreed upon weeks earlier and rush to renegotiate. As a result, they controlled the negotiations and influenced the outcome in their favor.

This brings me to my next point. Try to negotiate everything at one sitting. It is too easy to go back and renegotiate issues you have already agreed to if you don't sign the contract right away. As I said before, I now bring a laptop computer to the negotiations. It has all my contract clauses on it and, as we talk, I type it in the contract, pulling up the clauses I need. When we are done with the negotiation, I print out the contract and all the parties sign it. This way, in one sitting, the parties enter into a contract. No one changes his mind, no one can go back on a promise, and no one has time to think about it. This is a very powerful negotiation tool.

This tactic is particularly useful when you are in a negotiation where someone is making a lot of promises.

You ask: "Does the computer do this"?

Of course they say: "Absolutely".

How many times have you had a promise made by someone only to be told later that he never made that promise? Now, every time someone makes me a promise I write it down and add it to the warranty part of the contract. (A warranty is simply a promise that you rely on. We will be talking about warranties later in this book). Suddenly, the other side sees it, and backtracks on its position. You know right away if the other party has not been completely honest with you. Getting it in writing also holds the party to its promises and can influence the balance of power in your negotiation.

Another powerful negotiation tool is listening. We all love to hear ourselves talk and often feel that if we talk enough we can persuade the other side to give in to our point of view. Remember, when you are talking you are not listening. If someone is talking to you while you are talking do you think he is hearing a word you say, no.

You need to listen to the other side and make sure they listen to you as well. The negotiation needs to be controlled, and he who controls the negotiation gets the power. The better prepared you are for the negotiation the better you will be able to listen. Sometimes you have a problem where one side is not talking clearly and you cannot determine their position. As a result, you must ask questions of the other side: "Where are you getting that figure", and "What is the basis for your opinion"? By asking questions like these you are showing you are reasonable, and it opens a dialog between the sides.

Stage Two

The second stage in an effective negotiation is establishing the opening cost or price. You need to decide on your opening offer before you ever talk to the other side. How many times have you been asked, "How much are you willing to pay", only to be left thinking that you really didn't know the answer to the question? You also must know what you want included for that price. Take for example the situation one company found after purchasing a computer system. During the negotiations for a computer system things went far better than expected. In fact, the company was getting each and every item they asked for and seemed amazed at what a pushover the seller had been. Then the system was delivered.

The computer system came in a hundred pieces. Not only did the people have no idea how to assemble the computer system, they had no idea how to use it once the system was assembled and up and running. The computer company was happy to provide assistance, of course, at premium prices. The buyer failed to consider everything that was involved in implementing the computer system and to include those items in the calculations of price he was willing to pay.

When negotiating for price, you do not want to open up with a price that is too close to your ideal price because you will not have much room to bargain. Also, you don't want to set your opening price too low because it will make you seem unreasonable. Instead, you must do some research and make an educated decision about how to open. In our example with the oranges, let's assume our research showed there had been a good harvest and the supplier sold the same quantity of oranges to another purchaser for $3.80 a pound. Here a good opening price could be $3 a pound.

Stage Three

The third stage in effective negotiations is finding the range. There is no such thing as one ideal price. Every fair price has a range. Both you and the supplier probably have a range that you consider to be acceptable. Depending on how much of a price you are negotiating, your range can be large or small. You must determine the range for each side and use that range effectively in your negotiation process. This leads to Stage Four.

Stage Four

You need to do research about the company. There are several factors involved in researching a company. Start early and be comprehensive. Look at public information on the company. Stock prices, annual reports, newspaper articles, social media, etc. can give you important information. Look at the company's track record. Talk to the company's suppliers, competitors and employees. This type of information will tell you a lot about how your negotiation is going to proceed and will help you in determining how you are going to handle the negotiation process.

In Stage Four you find the overlap of the two ranges. You look for the point at which both you and the supplier will be satisfied. A large part of your power comes from your command of the information available to you. He with the most information has the most power and can drive the best bargain. In negotiations, knowledge is power. Finding the overlap sounds easy but it can be very difficult, especially if you are talking about more things than just cost. What if you are negotiating a contract that will have fifty points? Some things you would be willing to give up and some things you absolutely need or you will not go through with the deal.

Performing a MIL analysis is important when planning your negotiation.

MIL is an acronym and stands for:

MUST achieve

INTEND to achieve

Would LIKE to achieve

You can take the elements of your contract and rate them for both yourself and your supplier. This way you can find out what is important to each of you. For example, you can rate:

- Date of delivery

- Quality

- Limitation of Liability

- Remedy

- Warranty

- Insurance

- Price

- Payment

You perform an MIL analysis by listing each of the goals in your negotiation. You then decide whether it is a must achieve, intend to achieve or would like to achieve for each side. You also need to decide if each goal is something you're willing to give up, or in the alternative, if there are things you will be willing to give up to achieve your goal. You should note that some items on the list obviously have more weight for you and some items on the list obviously have more weight for your supplier.

Never give up anything in a negotiation without receiving something for it. Let's say that you are negotiating for the delivery of a new part. You don't care what color the part is because it is never going to be seen by anyone. That doesn't mean color should not be part of your negotiation. Perhaps you can get added concessions by telling the other side you can take whatever color they have. The point is, don't give it up without using it to your advantage. It gives you power in the negotiation.

You should never be afraid to walk away from a negotiation. Sometimes retreat really is the best option. Let's say you are in a negotiation and someone is really getting the best of you. You seem to be giving up every important point and not getting anything for your side. Well, run to that meeting you have. Return that important phone call. Do what is necessary to get up and take a break, whether it is just to clear your head or to leave the negotiation and come back another day. By walking away, you are controlling the process and once again taking some of the power for yourself.

Power can come from many sources among them:

- Knowledge

- Honesty

- Risk Taking

- Partnerships

- Planning

- Attitude

Each of the items listed above gives you power if you have it and use it correctly. However, using one incorrectly may cause you to lose your power and give it to the other side.

Often, one side will try to use deadlines as a tactic to get power. For example, you are told they need an answer by tomorrow or they cannot make a deal. This tactic is a favorite of the car salesperson. He tells you that you have this great price for the car but only if you buy the car today. He uses this to try to force an agreement out of you. In software, they use the recognition of revenue to move the deal along faster. Remember, that is a concession. The date you will make a decision is one of your bargaining points and something you should have planned for in your negotiation process.

How do you handle a deadline? First, be patient, if you allow a deadline to upset you, you are losing power and giving the other side the upper hand in your negotiation. Second, always try to find out if it is a real deadline or an arbitrary one. Sometimes deadlines are real. For example, you are buying oranges, and in time they will spoil. Or, you are competing against another buyer for the same purchase. Again, knowledge is power.

Lastly, look for creative approaches to solve deadlines. You can attack the deadline and not the contract issues. A deadline is just another issue to negotiate.

Remember, you can also use deadlines to your benefit. Tell the other side that you need an answer by a certain date. I have even gone as far as to offer a certain amount with a deadline for response. Then when the other party doesn't agree before the deadline has past, I give them a new amount, one that is less attractive, with another deadline. If they don't agree by that deadline, I make an offer that is even less attractive. If you can pull it off it is a very effective negotiation tactic.

Finally, remember that deadlines are almost always arbitrary. They aren't real. Don't worry about it. Deadlines are only for the benefit of the person placing the deadline. If you're not ready, don't worry. The deal should still be there later. If not, it probably wasn't meant to be.

Stage Five

The final stage in the negotiation process is reaching an agreement. Obviously, this is the most difficult stage of the negotiation process. Partnership is the goal of every negotiation, and you need to work together. This is very difficult for many reasons. I cannot stress enough the importance of negotiating as much as possible up front. Leave nothing to chance and never assume that everyone thinks something is as obvious as you do.

Problems also arise when one side is afraid to bring up a point because they know it is going to be a problem. Don't wait until the last minute to bring up a point that may be the subject of some disagreement. Bring it up early. If you wait until the end to talk about the most difficult subject, the negotiation may break down because you have nothing left to talk about. If you discuss the topic early you can agree to disagree for the time being and come back to the topic later. Maybe you or the other side can trade something and get a concession on the point you had disagreed about.

Reaching an agreement on all points of a contract is not the end. The contract still needs to be written, and that means agreeing to all contract clauses that were created.

Until we tell lawyers to write in plain English, contracts will always seem like a foreign language. People must take charge of their lawyers. Not only do you have to negotiate with the other side, but with lawyers as well. You've agreed to everything and then look at the contract to find it totally different. You never even talked about where you can file a lawsuit if something goes wrong. But looking at the contract, you see a clause stating that any lawsuit must be brought in Alaska. Who wants to go to Alaska to sue someone? Now, suddenly, you are negotiating again.

Once you reached an agreement you need to close the deal quickly: reduce the agreement to writing and sign it. Remember, until you sign the agreement, everything is still open to negotiation, even if you have previously agreed to the items.

Elements of a Successful Negotiation

First and foremost, a contract must provide you with reliability over a period of time. You must be able to rely on delivery dates, quality, costs and other factors. The whole point of entering into an agreement is so you do not have to think about these things all the time. Second, a partnership is based upon the fact that there is a long-term commitment to working together. Not only must you follow the terms of the agreement, you must also work together if a problem arises. You want to feel good about the contract you've entered into. It should be a piece of paper that you sign and never have to take out again. Finally, a partnership means that information and data are shared. There are open communication lines. To some this may seem like a marriage and, in a way, that's what a contract is. It is a marriage between two sides for their mutual benefit.

Again, if you do not have a good negotiation, you cannot have a good contract.

CONTRACT REQUIREMENTS

CHAPTER FOUR

For some, this is going to be the most boring chapter in the book. WAIT!! Don't skip ahead to Chapter Five. The weird thing about this book is that everything in it builds upon everything else. You have to understand this to understand what we are going to talk about later. How can we discuss contracts when you don't even know what they are? So, you need to read this chapter and understand the basics.

This chapter focuses on the basics of contract law. This book, one of a series I will be doing for purchasing professionals, gives you the basics in a short period of time. It is by no means comprehensive. Law school students study the material in this chapter in-depth for a full year. Also, as every lawyer will tell you, the law is constantly changing, and laws can vary from state to state. So, keep that in mind. However, the basic elements of a contract never change. These include:

- Offer

- Acceptance

- Consideration

Is There an Offer?

An offer is a promise to do something now or to refrain from doing something in the future. It also creates in the offeree, the person receiving the offer, the power of acceptance. The offeree now has the choice to accept or reject the offer that was made.

Some things are not offers. Inquiries, bartering, expressions of opinion, preliminary negotiations, advertisements, catalogs and so forth are all not offers.

Let's say that a man goes to a grocery store and buys a can of corn for 45 cents. That's a contract. Money was paid for corn, and corn was sold. What was the offer? Some would say the offer was the can of corn on the shelves of the store. So when the man picked up the can of corn, he accepted the offer and formed a contract. That is not the case. The offer actually occurs when the man goes to the cash register and offers to buy the corn. Acceptance occurs when the store employee takes the money and thus agrees to sell the corn.

What if a woman saw an ad in the newspaper that advertised the corn for a penny a can? When she gets to the store, however, there is no corn for a penny – it is all 85 cents. Can the woman get the corn for a penny? She would argue that the advertisement is an offer, and when she went to the store to purchase the corn she was accepting the offer. The truth is that, as a general rule, price quotations and advertisements are not offers but only preliminary negotiations, which solicit offers from others.

The only way around this is if there are items known as "goods identified to the contract". That means the seller must promise to definitely sell a certain good that you can precisely identify. For example, someone put an ad in the paper stating he will sell his 1995 BMW for $500. There was a picture of it so you would know the exact car he wanted to sell. This is an offer. You know exactly what is up for sale and how much it costs. Generally, the more specific an advertisement is, the more likely it is to be considered an offer. Automobile dealers who advertise with a picture of a car get around this by saying the price is only for "the car in the ad". The car you look at, of course, will be different.

There are four requirements for an offer that we can look at: present intent, definiteness, a serious intention and communication. Let's look at each of these requirements. First the offeror, the person making the offer, must want to enter into a valid contract now. If the offeror says, "I will be selling my car tomorrow for $500", that is not an offer. If there is not present intent, there is no offer, and it is nothing more than an advertisement.

Even if the parties have intent to enter into an agreement right now, the agreement made between the parties cannot be indefinite. Performance is defined as how each party will behave under an agreement. The concept of definiteness tells us that the performance of the parties must be so definite that each party knows exactly what they are getting out of the deal. This does not mean that every single item must be agreed to by the parties. Gap fillers, which we will cover later, can fill in things that the parties have not discussed. As a basic rule we must be definite as to the parties in the contract, the subject matter of the contract, the price of the subject matter and the time of performance.

An offer must be serious. Many times we hear someone say he/she will sell you something for a dollar. People are not always serious about these proposed sales. If a person offers to sell you his Jaguar automobile for a dollar, he or she is probably not serious. Maybe he is just upset that his car broke down and is trying to convey that notion by saying he wants to get rid of the car. Once again we apply the reasonable person standard and examine whether or not a reasonable person would consider something to be an offer. How obvious was it that the offeror was making a joke?

So, reasonableness also helps determine what constitutes a serious offer. We are going to talk a lot in this book about reasonableness. It is a standard constantly applied by courts. Reasonableness examines how a reasonable person behaves. For example, if a reasonable person would consider something to be an offer then, most likely, it will be. Obviously, this is not an easy standard to apply. In fact, we hope we never have to get to that point.

Jokes are not the only things that keep an offer from being serious. Offers made in anger or fear, are also not considered offers. However, in these cases an offeree must be aware of the anger or the fear or the fact that the offeror was making a joke. Did the offeror show that he wanted to be obligated to do something?

The final element of an offer is communication. Until the offeror communicates the offer to the offeree, there is no intent to be bound or obligated to do anything. Most offers are communicated face to face, email, or through the mail. But, what if someone sends an offer letter and it never was received? Then, of course, there never was an offer because the offeree never received it.

Offers can be terminated in one of three ways. First, an offer can be terminated because of a lapse of time. For example, a real estate offer contains a time of acceptance clause. The offer specifically says, "This offer will remain open until…" and gives a specific date. Obviously, after that date the offer is terminated, unless the parties mutually agree to extend the offer. If no time is stated in the offer it is open for a reasonable time or until the offeror revokes the offer.

Prior to acceptance by the offeree, an offeror is always free to change his mind. Of course, the offeror must communicate the revocation to the offeree, and the offeree must, in fact, receive notice that the offer has been terminated. The offeree can also reject the offer, indicating that he does not want to enter into a contract with the offeror. But, what happens if the offeror offers to sell his car for $1200 and the offeree offers to pay $1000 instead? This leads to acceptance.

Is There Acceptance?

Acceptance is the second requirement for a contract. For our purposes, we can define acceptance as agreement to an offer. To determine whether there is acceptance several items need to be addressed. For an acceptance to be valid it must be voluntary. Someone cannot be forced to accept the offer. There also must be some overt act by which the offeree manifests intent to accept the offer. The acceptance must be communicated to the offeror and must mirror the offer. Finally, the acceptance must come from the offeree.

Both the offer and the subsequent acceptance must be voluntary, referring to the fact that an offeree must accept the offer of his own free will, not under duress. Duress is a legal concept which states that if a person is forced to enter into a contract it is unenforceable. For example, someone holds a gun to your head and makes you sign a contract, obviously, you should not be held to that agreement.

However, what if you are going bankrupt and, as a result, you are being forced to sell your home? Some would say that you are under duress and should not be held to that contract. Economic pressure or other types of pressure are not necessarily duress. As a general rule, if some act by another person overcomes your free will that is considered duress.

As we have stated already, the courts use a reasonable person standard: would a reasonable person in your place feel threatened and forced to enter into the agreement? It is not simply that you feel duress; it is whether or not a reasonable person does. Undue influence, which occurs when someone puts pressure on you as a result of his or her position, falls into the same category as duress.

To accept an offer there must also be an intention to accept the offer, and that intention must be shown in an act by the offeree. The offeree must promise to act in the future or he must perform. When we buy a house we promise to perform and that performance shows that we accept the offer.

Can silence be acceptance? For example, what if I say that I will sell you my car for $100,000 and if I do not hear from you by 5 o'clock tomorrow I will consider you to have accepted my offer and will send the car over? As a general rule, silence does not constitute acceptance. However, as always with general rules, there are always exceptions. Prior history may provide a basis for silence to be treated as acceptance. For example, in your dealings with supplier XYZ, he always shipped the parts if he did not hear from you. In that case, your silence will be considered acceptance.

Mirror Image Rule

Now we come to the mirror image rule. This rule states that the acceptance must mirror the offer in every way. Acceptance cannot change any part of the offer or it is considered a counteroffer, which in turn, must be accepted by the new offeree.

In the case of the $1200 car, the former offeree has, in effect, rejected the offer and made an offer of his own at $1000.

Let's look at a situation where an offeror says that he will sell you 16" green widgets for $1 a widget and ship the widgets on July 28 to your warehouse in Miami. Your acceptance must mirror each and every point in the offer or there is not an acceptance. This means you must agree that:

1.   you will buy

2.   16"

3.   green

4.   widgets

5.   at $1 a piece

6.   shipped

7.   to your warehouse

8.   in Miami

9.   on July 28.

If you change any provision of the offer, it is not an acceptance; it is a counteroffer, which must be accepted by the new offeree. An exception to this rule occurs where someone says that he does not want to accept the offer but he will accept it anyway. Just because they don't like your offer that does not mean the acceptance is any less valid.

What if the person accepts the offer on all of the nine points listed above but asks how the widgets will be shipped: by boat or Federal Express? Obviously, this makes a big difference in the deal. But, it has not been covered by the offer. Generally, this change will not affect the fact that you have accepted the offer. It will be considered a request for an addition to the agreement and will either be accepted or rejected, by itself, by the offeror.

Of course, this depends on how you state this addition. You can say it two ways:

"I accept your offer, but I want them shipped Federal Express".

Or

"I want them shipped Federal Express if we are going to go ahead with the deal".

Obviously, in the first case there is more likely an acceptance than in the second case. As with all things in the law, most of the time the answer is: "It depends on the facts of your situation". I cannot stress enough how "case-sensitive" purchasing law is. The answer to any question can change with a difference in one fact. I must reiterate the fact that nothing in this book is cast in stone.

An offeror can make the acceptance contingent upon a certain fact. For example, what if an offeror states in his offer that to accept the offer you must go to the town hall and stand on your head at noon? That seems ridiculous for that to be considered acceptance. However, common law states that if the offer tells you an exclusive way you must state your acceptance, you must do exactly that for there to be an acceptance. The standing on your head essentially becomes another term of the contract that must be accepted by you for you to accept the offer. The Uniform Commercial Code does away with the requirement of a specific way to accept and states that acceptance can be manifested in any commercially reasonable manner. In other words, a phone call, a letter or email all can be considered ways to accept an offer.

Acceptance must come from the offeree. Let's assume three people are at a table: Jones, Smith and Green. Jones offers to sell his watch to Green for fifty dollars. Smith cannot accept the offer because it was not made to him; only Green can accept the offer. If Smith says that he will buy the watch it is merely an offer, which must in turn, be accepted by Jones.

In most cases, offers will remain open until one of two things happen: either the offeror revokes the offer or the offeree rejects or accepts the offer. Up until the offeree accepts or rejects the offer, the offeror can revoke his offer. Revoke means that the offeror can change his mind and withdraw the offer. The general rule of thumb is that the offeror can revoke the offer at any time prior to acceptance by the offeree. Of course, once the offeree has accepted the offer, a contract is formed, and the offer cannot be revoked.

In some cases an offer cannot be revoked. The Uniform Commercial Code uses this example: if a buyer or seller states in a written document that the offer will be held open for a reasonable period of time and then signs the document, the offer cannot be revoked. We also see the example where the offeror gets money for holding the offer open. For example, you pay the offeror $100 to keep the offer open for ten days. You lose your hundred dollars in exchange for the ten days. What we have in those cases is essentially a mini-contract where one side has offered to keep the offer open for a certain amount of time in exchange for money and the other has agreed to pay money in exchange for the time.

An offer will end if an offeree rejects the offer or if the offeree makes a counteroffer. Just as there are many ways to make an offer, there are many ways to reject an offer as well. The easiest way is for the offeree to say, "I reject your offer". As with the offer, this rejection must be communicated to the offeror. However, this is not what happens in most cases. Instead, the offeree most likely says that he would like to change something in the offer and then he will accept it. In many cases, this exchange of offer and counteroffer goes back and forth until the parties come to some agreement on the terms of the deal.

Is There Consideration?

Having discussed offer and acceptance, this brings us to the third element of a contract: consideration. Even if an offer and acceptance exist this does not mean there is a contract. You still need consideration, i.e. value exchanged for a promise. This exchanging of value means that each side must be giving something up in the bargain. It is the exchange of value, one side to the other that makes the promise enforceable.

Both parties must give something up. Each side must have a legal benefit (where a party does something she/he would not normally have to do or refrain from something, she/he has a legal right to do). Both sides must each do this and bind themselves to do those things through an offer and acceptance. I offer to sell you my home for $100,000. Let's assume you agree to buy the home from me for the $100,000. In that case, you have promised to receive the home (your legal benefit), and you have promised to pay $100,000 (your legal detriment). I have agreed to sell you the home (my legal detriment) and to receive the $100,000 (my legal benefit).

This consideration is exchanged between the parties, and this exchange must be bargained for. In other words, you must bargain to give up something you normally would be entitled to. If you have to do it anyway it is not consideration. The amount of consideration is not an issue. If you have ever looked at a deed to a home or the beginning of many contracts you will see a clause that says something like:

"...for $10 and other valuable consideration herein deemed to have been given and received by and between the parties..."

This is a standard clause in many contracts that gets around the requirements of consideration. It says you have exchanged, among other things, $10. This way you never have to deal with consideration because the contract states that you have exchanged consideration that is bargained for and sufficient.

Not only does the use of this clause ensure your contract covers consideration, it also eliminates the worry over putting the actual price in the contract. What if you are buying someone's car for $50? It is a great bargain, but you don't want to tell anyone how much you are paying. You don't want the competition to know. On the other hand, you have to tell people that there is consideration. That is another reason why we use the clause.

The amount of consideration generally is not an issue. If the parties bargain for it and agree to the amount of consideration it is usually sufficient.

Offer. Acceptance. Consideration. Those are the basic elements you will need for a contract. Yet contracts are much more complex than simply these three elements. Life is more complex than ever. And living in a litigious society, our contracts have grown along with us. Simply knowing those three elements is not going to help you. In the next chapter we will be discussing more specific elements of a contract. In particular, what clauses you want in a contract and why.

OTHER CONTRACT ELEMENTS

CHAPTER FIVE

Offer, acceptance and consideration are not the only things you need to know about contracts. Obviously, contracts contain many other elements that we need to discuss. Additionally, we need to consider whether or not people can even enter into a contract. This chapter will provide you with a basis for beginning to draft contracts. We also look at clauses you will need to know about in order to enter into agreements.

Most of us know that contracts do not necessarily have to be in writing. I offer to sell you my computer for $100. You say, "yes". We then exchange money and the computer. Nothing is ever written down. But, when can we have a verbal contract, and when do we need to reduce that contract to writing?

To prevent fraudulent promises, the Statute of Frauds states that certain contracts must be in writing to be enforceable by a court. The Statute of Frauds lists three types of contracts that must be in writing:

- Contracts for land

- Contracts that cannot be performed within one year

- Contracts for the sale of goods over $500

In each case, we can see the need to have the contracts written. We need to be able to look at the contract and rely on that writing so we have certainty over time. For contracts involving the purchase of land, you want to be able to track and record those purchases in public records for title searches and other investigations to ensure a buyer can purchase the property. If these contracts were not in writing, how could we ever be sure who owned the property?

For contracts that cannot be performed within a year we need reliability over the course of the agreement. Since the contract will last for an extended period of time, we want to make sure people do not forget the details of their agreements. People have a lot on their minds. Sometimes we can't remember what we did last week, let alone all the details of the agreement we entered into eighteen months ago. Because of this we require people to write the contract down so that they can refer to it in the future.

Contracts, which are over $500, are also required to be in writing for specific reasons. Since these contracts involve large sums of money, they must be in writing. Again, we want people to be able to rely on these agreements to protect themselves.

So, a contract has to be in writing, but how detailed does the writing need to be? If I take a napkin and write: "I am selling you my car for $5000", sign the napkin and give it to you, is that sufficient for us to form a contract? Most contracts contain many additional elements, which we will discuss later in this book. However, even though those elements are not in the writing above, that writing does satisfy the minimal requirements of a contact.

To satisfy the minimal writing requirements, a contract must have the following items:

- Quantity

- Identification of the parties

- Signature of either party

The basic contract is simple: just jot down the most important elements of the deal and sign your name to the contract. Even a complete signature is not necessary ... signing an "X" instead of a full signature is not enough to get you out of the contract.

Today, it's not that people do not want to write a contract down. It is just the opposite. People not only want to have a written contract they want to be the ones to write the contract. You have a law firm; they have a law firm. We send contracts and purchase orders back and forth between the both of us. I send you a purchase order with some terms;

you send me a confirmation with totally different terms. When there are several writings each with different terms and conditions what do we do?

My first piece of advice is the same not just in this situation, but in any situation where you are talking to the other side in a contract or negotiation situation: write the other side and determine what you are going to do about the situation. Do not just assume the other side thinks the same thing you do. You may not think that their confirmation contains the correct terms. So send the other side a letter informing them you will not be going by the terms in the confirmation and if they do not agree, they need to notify you immediately in writing. This will protect both of you in case of a disagreement. A record of the writing is important for you to retain, especially if you are having subordinates write the letters on your behalf.

Confidentiality Agreements

Before contact negotiations begin you need to consider the need for a confidentiality agreement to protect sensitive information. A confidentiality agreement is executed separately from your general purchasing contract. Why?

Think about it. If you have confidential items that you do not want disclosed, when is the time to sign a contract to protect them? Should you wait until the final contract? That is certainly not the case. By the time the final contract is signed, all of your corporate secrets have already been disclosed. They are, therefore, public knowledge and not subject to protection.

You need to sign the confidentiality agreement first, well before any contract negotiations take place. Certainly sign one before you disclose any confidential information to the other side. In brief, a confidentiality agreement states that any disclosures by either company, which by their very nature, are confidential shall be kept secret by the other side for a period of x years.

It is important that you define what "confidential" will mean.

You may need to mark items as "confidential" with a stamp. Or, you may want to list those items, which you know will be confidential. In the agreement you will at least want to state that the copyrights and patents your company has obtained will not be infringed upon by the other side. You will also need to put in your contract those remedies you will be entitled to in the case of a breach of the confidentiality agreement.

Parole Evidence Rule

What do you do in the case where you have a contract and then someone tries to change the terms of the contract because of your prior negotiations. For example, I am going to buy pencils from you, and we enter into an agreement where I will buy $50,000 worth of pencils over the next year. We talked about the manner of delivery, and I stated I wanted the pencils boxed 100 to a box. You, as the seller, stated that 500 to a box are standard. The contract is silent on the manner of delivery. Can I demand the pencils come 100 to a box?

The Parole Evidence Rule states that if two or more parties have a contract and express the contract, in writing, and if the writing is a complete and accurate expression of the agreement of the parties, then any evidence of anything prior to the formation of the contract will not be admitted for the purpose of varying the writing. The courts have stated that if you wanted a term in the contract, you would have put it in there. The fact that you left it out of the agreement tells us something.

It is a basic tenant of contract law that the court seeks to enforce the contract. However, in this case, the parties are disputing the terms. First, the Parole Evidence Rule states that the court will not even hear evidence if you are going to contradict the writing in the contract. The court assumes you negotiated and settled for what is in the contract. But what if the case we talked about where the manner of delivery of the pencils is not in the contract?

In that case the Parole Evidence Rule states that an agreement may be explained or supplemented by evidence of consistent additional terms, or to explain an agreement by course of dealing, course of performance or usage of trade. We can bring in evidence as to terms that do not contradict what is in the contract. The important thing for the court to consider is whether or not the contract was meant to be the final expression of the parties' agreement. The Uniform Commercial Code covers these elements of the Statute of Frauds in Section 2-202.

As you can see, this can create a lot of legal problems. We are going to have to go to court and fight over several things:

- Is the contract a final expression of our agreement?

- Are there additional or different terms from those in the contract?

- Do the other elements apply (such as a course of dealing between the parties)?

We do not want to have to do these things. Instead, most contracts contain something called an entire agreement clause:

"This agreement constitutes a final written expression of all the terms of the agreement and is a complete and exclusive statement of those terms".

If we used this clause in a contract in our pencil example, than what was written in the contract becomes final. Our discussions regarding 100 or 500 to a box do not matter. However, since the contract is silent on this matter, the standard form of delivery, 500 to a box, will most likely apply.

This clause helps to avoid risk because it tells everyone that if something is not in the agreement we do not care because it was not supposed to be included. You are put on notice: if you think it is important, make sure it is in the contract. For companies doing business through sales people, the clause gains added significance. If my sales person makes you a promise, and it is not in the contract, this clause prevents you from trying to use it against me later. When we talk about warranties we will discuss sales people's promises from the buyer's point of view.

Agency Law

Agency law is an essential element in understanding contracts. An agent is any person who is authorized to act under someone else's direction or control and for the benefit of third parties. The principal is the person who directs the activities of the agent. Any buyer is an agent of the company. However, in many cases the agent may not have authority to perform certain types of transactions. For example, a company may have Buyer One, Buyer Two and Buyer Three. Each buyer can purchase different amounts. Buyer One can purchase anything up to $10,000. Buyer Two can purchase anything up to $100,000. Buyer Three can purchase anything up to $1,000,000. Thus the authority of the various buyers, the agents, is dependent upon how much they can purchase.

In the case I just illustrated the agents are general agents, agents who are authorized to transact any and all business of a particular kind. A principal is liable for any act of his general agent. This applies even if the agent did not have the actual authority to perform a particular act. Because a general agent has the apparent authority to conduct transactions and because another person does not know what the buyer can and cannot do, the responsibility is put on the principal to make sure the other party knows the limits of the agent's authority.

A special agent, on the other hand, has limited authority to act for the principal in only one specific transaction. If a special agent exceeds his authority, the principal may not be liable. However, it is important that a special agent's authority be clearly identified.

In the case of Buyer One, she can only purchase up to $10,000. If she purchases $15,000 that transaction will probably be upheld by a court because someone else may not know exactly how much Buyer One could purchase. Therefore, it is very important for a principal to notify third parties as to the limits of the agent's authority. If an unauthorized agent is transacting business on behalf of a company, it is up to the principal to immediately notify the suppliers. Otherwise, the company will be held to those transactions.

An agent has several duties to a principal. First, an agent must act in good faith. There can be no secret kickbacks from suppliers and no advantages that the agent grants suppliers. Second, an agent must be obedient to the desires of the principal. The agent must follow the directions of the principal as to what he can and cannot do. Third, an agent must exercise reasonable care, skill and diligence in the performance of his duties. What reasonable care, diligence and skill are depends upon the situation. Fourth, an agent is responsible for an accounting to the principal. An agent must give the principal what is due him. In essence, there is a contract between the principal and the agent to do certain things and the agent must fulfill those functions. The final responsibility of the agent is to give the principal information as to his or her activities and to report facts and opinions.

A principal also has duties to the agent. First, an agent must be compensated for the duties he or she performs. The dollars paid to the agent essentially form the basis for a mini-contract between the principal and the agent. The agent gets the money and, in exchange, performs services on behalf of the principal. Second, a principal must reimburse his agent for expenses, which the agent incurs on the principal's behalf. Finally, the principal must indemnify the agent for her/his acts. The indemnification occurs so long as the agent is properly performing her/his duty and, as a result of the performance of these duties, becomes liable to a third party. Thus, if an agent sells a piece of equipment, the principal must indemnify the agent for any damages which are incurred because the agent was acting at the direction of the principal.

There are a few important lessons here for anyone who is dealing with agents. Obviously, you must know exactly the limits of the agent's authority. Can the agent transact with you the business that is being proposed? Of course, it assumes as well, that the agent knows his or her authority. I cannot tell you how many times I have gone to a settlement conference only to see that the person on the other side of the table does not have the authority to settle the case. He has to call someone else. As I have said before, there is no point in talking to this person. He is not, in fact, an agent of the principal, as far as I am concerned, because he/she cannot get the job done. If you are dealing with the wrong person you need to make a change.

Another word of warning, this time for when dealing with an agent who you are not sure is acting with the best interests of the principal in mind. If an agent appears to be acting adversely to his/her principal, you are dealing with the agent at your own risk. You should contact the principal in this case and investigate the agent's authority and decide whether or not you should be dealing with this person.

Purchasing Cards

I want to take some time here to discuss one of the trends in purchasing: purchasing cards. These cards are very popular right now. Purchasing cards are charge cards for people in Purchasing to use in the course of their jobs. These cards have several advantages:

• They allow purchases without going through your accounting department for approval prior to purchase.

• They allow you to create hierarchies in your company of who can purchase what goods and services.

• They allow for easy tracking of buying.

• You have buyer protection for unwanted purchases.

• Certain items or amounts can be blocked to prevent inappropriate purchases.

However, there are several drawbacks to purchasing cards as well:

• There is no supervision for all purchases.

• They can be stolen and used by unauthorized personnel.

• They may be overused.

People in the purchasing field love purchasing cards because these cards make a buyer's job easier, especially those who frequently make small purchases. But you must be careful. By giving these cards to the agents of your company you are authorizing these unknown purchases. While you can return those unwanted goods, you will have to look at each and every purchase and that may be more difficult. So be careful when using purchasing cards to make sure the benefits outweigh the drawbacks.

Terms of a Contract

Some of the terms of a contract are obvious: price, quantity, delivery, etc. However, courts may apply other terms not expressly written in your contract based on various factors. The UCC mentions several such factors. First, the court may look to a course of dealing between the parties, i.e. how the parties have behaved prior to executing this agreement. Let's use the pencil example. Even before buying pencils from you I knew they came 500 pencils to a box. This will influence the court because I knew they came that way and did not change it in the contract. The court will imply the term 500 pencils per box.

The court will also provide terms based upon usage of the trade, which answers the question: How do other people in the industry view this transaction? In essence, we are attempting to imply terms based upon the reasonable person standard.

Finally, terms may be applied based upon a course of performance, which deals with what has happened after we signed the agreement. How have we behaved under this contract? You always shipped pencils to me in 100 pencil boxes, and I always accept the pencils, it will be difficult for me later to claim the contract said I was to receive 500 pencils per box.

Gap Fillers

It seems obvious that a contract would have terms like quantity, quality, price and delivery schedule. But what happens if one of these terms is not in the agreement. It would seem to some like a big mistake, so the contract should be thrown out because important terms like price or quality were forgotten. The terms that are left out of a contract are called "gaps" which are created for a variety of reasons, some by mistake and some on purpose. The UCC has various gap filler provisions, which discuss what to do if various terms are missing.

The first gap filler is based upon delivery terms. The UCC states that unless the parties agree, the time of delivery shall be a reasonable time. Obviously, we are going to have to negotiate to define "reasonable time". The place of delivery is generally the seller's place of business. If I buy a television set, I usually buy it at the store. Again, these provisions apply only if the contract does not specify these terms.

If payment terms are missing from the contract the UCC states that, as a general rule, payment is due at the time goods are delivered. The seller's release of the goods and receipt of the money happen at the same time. As a result, the contract is concluded and everyone moves on with their lives. A buyer may inspect the goods and reject nonconforming goods. Payment may be made in the form of a check, but if the check is not honored, the seller can come back and reclaim his goods. Thus, a check is not considered a final form of payment.

It seems unthinkable that the price term could be missing from an agreement. But what if that happens? Let's say I am buying the new T900 turbo grill for my backyard. It has yet to be produced. The grill is being custom built especially for me. You have no idea how much it will cost until you actually build the grill. Yet, we want to enter into a contract so I can buy the new grill. What do we do about price?

In such circumstances where the price is missing from a contract, the UCC implies a reasonable price. There will be negotiations and even possibly litigation to determine a reasonable price. In the case of the grill, the court would look at how much went into the building the grill and factor in a reasonable profit for the manufacturer. Obviously, the grill is being built especially for me, and I should assume that the price would be determined by how much it costs to build the grill.

There can also be a partial gap as to price. We do not know how much the price will be, but we do know how that price will be computed. The contract could state that the price will be determined based on the cost of all materials plus a 20% markup. Therefore, we know how the price will be computed. The contract may specify price limits. For example, the price shall not exceed $1,000. Many current long-term leases contain provisions that provide that the price of the lease in subsequent years will be increased by the cost of living index. The increase in price is not known at the time but you are put on notice that there will be such an increase.

A greater problem occurs when the quantity is left out of the contract. Just as we can see some cases where the price can be left out of a contract the same exists with a quantity. You and a seller may enter into a contract where you agree to buy all of your requirements from the seller. You do not know how much of the product you are going to buy; you do know that no matter how much you buy, you are going to purchase all of it from the seller. These are called requirement contracts. Most courts uphold these types of agreements even though they do not have a quantity. The court will look at the reasonableness of the request and the ability of the seller to provide the amount. To determine if the request is unreasonable the court looks to see if there is an unjustified increase or decrease in the requirements or if a withdrawal of either part is unjustified.

This illustrates the difficulty that exists in using gap fillers. The lesson to be learned here is simple; be as specific as possible in your contract. If you are uncertain as to a specific term in the contract, try to narrow it down as much as possible and put what you know in the contract. For example, if you don't know how to calculate the price, state the things you want to use in the calculation or set limits on the price. In short, even if you do not know a term, you should know enough to put a great deal about the term into the contract.

CHAPTER SIX

There are many federal laws which affect our duties and responsibilities under contracts, which we may enter into. In fact, far too many laws exist to cover in any one book and the law moves at such a rapid pace that any commentary concerning the law runs the risk of being outdated well before the book is printed. The Uniform Commercial Code (UCC) itself, the focus of this chapter, takes up hundreds of pages, not to mention the volumes written about it. Plus, law schools devote an entire course to the study of the UCC.

This section is meant simply to introduce you to some of the laws that affect contracts and to give you some guidance about whether or not you need to do more research. Consequently, we are just going to hit the high points and move on.

Uniform Commercial Code

The primary law affecting our responsibilities under contracts for the purchasing professional must be the Uniform Commercial Code. It is important to note that the UCC only deals with goods, not services. This means that the UCC will not affect contracts for services. But, what if your contract deals with both goods and services?

If a contract deals with both goods and services, we must look to see which represents the larger part of the contract. If goods are the larger part of the contract, the UCC will apply. If services are the larger part of the contract, the UCC will not apply. Of course, this may be a difficult determination to make. One indication may be the cost associated with both goods and services in the contract. Another indication may be the amount of time allotted in the contract. You can even state which predominates in your contract.

The Uniform Commercial Code has several sections dealing with everything from banking to the sale of goods. In this book I will address

Article 2, which talks about the sale of goods.

The UCC was meant to help people who formed contracts by providing guidance about what would happen in a variety of situations. Additionally, the UCC made it easier to form contracts and imposes obligations on each party that do not have to be spelled out in the contract. For example, we spoke earlier about the mirror image rule where the acceptance of an offer had to mirror the offer in every way in order to form the contract. This is no longer the case. All that matters according to the UCC is that the parties both intend to enter into a contract. Once that happens it is not necessary for the parties to agree on all the terms. So, even if the offer and acceptance do not match exactly, under the UCC you still have a contract on the terms on which you and the other party do agree. You can form the contract and work out the rest of the details later.

In the last Chapter, I discussed the concept of gap fillers. The UCC created gap fillers to ensure that if the two parties intended to form a contract, they will have a contract, even if they forget to include some essential terms. The UCC also discusses warranties, and the warranty section of the UCC has some of the most far-reaching effects on contracts.

Warranties

The best way to describe warranties is to give you an example. Janet goes to buy a computer system from Discount Computers. She asks the sales person what the computer can do. For example, she wants to make sure the computer does several things like run the programs she uses and interface with the hardware that exists in her office. The sales person wants, of course, to make the sale. He makes all kinds of promises to Janet about the computer. Of course, the computer can run all software. Of course, the computer will interface with all the hardware.

Based on the sales person's statements Janet decides to buy the computer. But how does she make sure she's really getting everything the sales person promised her? The answer lies in the world of warranties.

To protect herself, Janet could put a warranty in the contract.

A warranty is basically a written promise. We can put in the contract that "the Seller warrants that the computer system purchased will run with all existing software and will interface with existing hardware". However, we would have to list the software and hardware to prevent misunderstandings about what exactly the computer will have to do. This warranty we placed in the contract protects Janet if the sales person lied.

If what the seller's agent told us is not true, that constitutes a breach of warranty which allows us to get out of the contract or seek damages. I'll discuss breach of warranty later in this chapter and damages in Chapter Nine.

The UCC discusses warranties and divides warranties into two sections, express and implied. An express warranty is any promise the seller makes to you about the goods. The warranty is that the goods will live up to the promises that the person makes. That's exactly what we did in the example above. We put the sales person's promise in writing. If we use the sales person's statement to decide to make the contract, that statement then becomes the warranty.

However, a seller does not need to use the word warranty. If someone advertises on a product that it will "remove even the worst tarnish from silver", the person is making a warranty, and the product should perform as stated.

An express warranty can also be created by a model or sample. A person or company may rely on the model or sample as a basis for forming a contract to purchase more of those goods. Therefore, the new goods had better match those that were sent as a sample.

The Uniform Commercial Code also provides people with other warranties. These warranties are not express warranties. They are not the actual promises made with regard to goods. Instead, these are implied warranties that the drafters of the UCC felt everyone should have, and the most basic guarantees that should be given to the purchaser of a product. I will discuss two warranties:

- Merchantability

- Fitness for a particular purpose

The implied warranty of merchantability means that the goods must actually be sellable and not defective. To put it more simply, the goods must be of a merchantable quality. If the goods are not of a sufficient quality and that lack of quality causes damage to a purchaser, the Seller of those goods can be liable for the damage caused because there was an implied warranty that the goods would not be of a type to cause damage. We use the assumption that merchantable goods should not be defective.

Of course the definition of "merchantable" causes its own problems. Section 2-314(2) of the UCC defines merchantable as goods that are fit for the ordinary purpose for which they have been purchased. The specification stems from the need to distinguish the use of the word "purpose" under the implied warranty of merchantability from its use under the implied warranty of fitness for a particular purpose.

The implied warranty of fitness for a particular purpose states that where a seller knows of a special purpose for which the goods will be used and that the buyer is relying on the seller to furnish goods that will be suitable for that purpose, than the goods will fit that purpose. This warranty is especially useful when buyers purchase goods using Requests for Proposals (RFP). In an RFP we question the sellers as to whether or not their product can meet our needs. Of course, when the sellers tell us the goods will meet our demands sellers are, in effect, giving us an implied warranty.

If we buy the product and it does not conform to the requirements for which we purchased it, a breach of the implied warranty results and the seller may be liable. Remember, with an implied warranty the seller must have made some type of promise that the goods could conform to the buyer's needs. And the buyer, in turn, must have relied on that warranty.

If a breach of warranty occurs, either in an express or implied warranty, a buyer can recover damages as provided for in the Uniform

Commercial Code. We will cover damages in Chapter Nine.

Warranty Disclaimers

The creators of the UCC, in an attempt to be fair, thought of the seller as well. They could not give all the rights to the buyer. The UCC allows the seller to disclaim the warranties, both express and implied.

To properly disclaim a warranty the UCC requires several things:

- The disclaimer must be in writing.

- It must be CONSPICUOUS.

- It must be unequivocal.

- It cannot be contradicted.

Most of the time the disclaimer takes the following form:

"SELLER DISCLAIMS ALL WARRANTIES EXPRESS AND IMPLIED INCLUDING THOSE OF FITNESS FOR A PARTICULAR PURPOSE AND MERCHANTABILITY".

As you can see, the buyer and seller have conflicting goals in this case. The buyer wants many warranties that will protect him from a variety of situations. The seller wants to disclaim all warranties. What will happen in the contract really comes down to negotiating power. He who has the most power will get what he wants.

Most of the time we have no choice. Ever buy a computer program? The disks usually come packaged in a sealed envelope with a sticker over the seal. To open the disks you tear the sticker as you break the seal. Ever read the sticker? In effect, by opening the envelope, you are entering into a contract with the software seller. When you break the seal you are agreeing to the terms and conditions in the contract. One of the things you are most likely agreeing to is that the seller has disclaimed all of its warranties. In effect the software maker is telling you it does not stand behind its product, and there is no promise the product will do what it is supposed to do.

So, what is an innocent buyer to do?

First, let me say that if a seller disclaims its warranties that does not mean that if the product is bad the company will refuse to do anything about it. Despite disclaiming the warranties, sellers usually fix their broken products to create and maintain a good corporate image. If companies get a reputation for not standing behind their products, they will go out of business. If the company does stand by the disclaimer, courts can render a disclaimer unconscionable. If there is a way that the courts can stand behind the consumer they usually find a way to do it. Therefore, sellers tend to be careful about disclaiming their warranties. They usually offer a limited warranty on the product and stand behind what they sell.

Second, earlier in this book I discussed negotiations; the battle over warranties is really determined by who has the power to negotiate the best deal. Again some simple advice to follow: if a contract does not have what you want, do not sign it or at least know what you are getting yourself into.

Breaches of Warranty

There are three types of breaches that can be created.

- Minor

- Material

- Minor plus anticipatory repudiation

A minor breach is a small breach that does not affect the contract. For example, the seller was supposed to deliver 100 pieces of copper pipe and instead delivered 105. They delivered a few too many pieces of copper. Although that is technically a breach of the contract because they did not deliver the proper quantity, in reality it really doesn't matter. The buyer still got 100 pieces. We call the breach minor because the improper quantity does not impair the contract.

A material breach, on the other hand, is a breach that impairs the entire essence of the contract. What makes a material breach? The answer is surprising: whatever we want. In the contract you may have a definition section where you list those things that will be considered a material breach of the contract. For example, you can state that any breach of warranty is a material breach of the contract.

The final type of breach is a minor breach plus anticipatory repudiation. In this type of breach there is only a minor breach, but we anticipate that the entire value of the contract is going to be impaired. Most often this occurs in installment contracts, contracts for a series of deliveries over time. For example, the seller will sell and the buyer will buy 100 computer boards every week for the next ten weeks. There are actually ten small contracts, each for the delivery of 100 computer boards. These smaller contracts are actually for the delivery of 1000 boards.

Now, let's say the first week the computer boards are delivered perfectly by the seller, as well as in the second and third weeks. However, in the fourth week the boards come two days late. Certainly that is a breach of the contract. You may even have called late delivery a material breach of the contract. But, in installment contracts the late delivery only impairs the fourth installment and not the others. As a general rule, this is not to be considered a material breach. The exception for this is if the late delivery substantially impairs the value of the entire contract.

For example, let's say it is week six and the fourth, fifth and sixth shipments from the seller still have not arrived. You call the seller, and he cannot assure you that the goods will be in route in the near future. In this case, you anticipate that the breach will be material. It is not a material breach at this point. The goods are only slightly late. But, you do not foresee the goods coming in, and this will therefore impair the value of the entire contract. Based on the concept of anticipatory repudiation we can treat the entire contract as breached and find another source for the goods.

You will have to prove that not receiving these three

shipments impairs the entire contract. If so, you can stop those shipments and future shipments because this is a breach of the whole contract. Anticipatory repudiation means you think the remaining shipments will also be late.

Remember, in any case of breach of contract, you need to protect yourself. I cannot stress enough the need to cover yourself, by writing letters to the other side in the event of even the most minor breach. The first time the seller breaches the contract you need to inform that party of the breach. You should state in writing that you will be obtaining the goods from an alternate source and plan on holding the seller responsible for the breach of contract.

We already discussed warranties and how they are tied to the concept of a breach of contract. We also discussed the different types of breach of contract, and how breach of contract is tied to the concept of remedies. This means that once we call something a breach of contract we need to decide what our remedy for that breach will be. Again, that is up to you, and you will need to provide for remedies in your contract. We will discuss remedies later in the book.

Besides the Uniform Commercial Code, there are several other laws that impact contracts used by the purchasing professional. The Sherman Antitrust Act discusses restraints of trade and monopolies. Both the Clayton Act and the Robinson-Patman Act prohibit price discrimination. These laws work to prevent monopolies, as well as other restraints of trade from occurring.

The Sherman Act is intended to prevent practices which may create a monopoly or restrain trade by limiting competition or trade. The law requires that there be interstate commerce, meaning the prevention of competition must cross state lines. Two separate companies conspiring to drive a third company out of business would violate the Sherman Antitrust Act.

Let's say Company A and Company B work together and drive Company C out of business. The mere fact that Company A and Company B work together does not violate the Sherman Act. Companies work together all the time. The two companies must be committed, must conspire, to work together to some illegal end. An example of this is restraining trade. This is a very difficult distinction for courts. Two companies may work together to further their own interests. However, those interests cannot be to illegally drive out the competition.

The Robinson-Patman Act deals with the sale of goods. It states you cannot discriminate in price between different purchasers of like goods when the result of such discrimination is the creation of a monopoly or the reduction in competition. It is also unlawful to induce such discrimination or monopoly. In other words, you cannot treat like companies differently for the purpose of creating a monopoly of unfair competition.

Because the Sherman Act was too general, the Clayton Act was adopted. The Sherman Act simply said restraint of trade and unfair competition was bad. But, we needed guidance about what companies could and could not do. In an effort to provide the guidance, the Clayton Act was drafted. Its general premise is that competition is good and preventing that competition should therefore be stopped. Violating the Clayton Act therefore requires some type of lease, sale or contract. Take Section 3 of the Clayton Act for example. Very simply put, it states that any person engaged in commerce may not make a contract or fix a price or give a discount where its effect is to lessen competition or create a monopoly. Generally we're talking about three types of agreements:

- Exclusive dealing agreements

- Requirement contracts

- Tying arrangements

Exclusive dealing agreements occur where two companies agree only to deal with each other and as a result exclude others from competition. The purpose of this exclusive dealing agreement must be to limit competition.

Requirement contracts are contracts which state you must purchase all your requirements from one source in order to make any purchase. In essence, they are seeking to lock you into one source and limit the ability of anyone else to compete against them by taking you as a client.

A tying agreement is one in which the parties agree that you can buy Product A from your supplier only if you buy Product B. Look at the antitrust lawsuit brought against the software giant Microsoft. The lawsuit alleged that for computer manufacturers to install the Windows 95 operating system on their computers Microsoft forced them to also install the Microsoft Internet Explorer. The computer manufacturers argue that Internet Explorer is a stand-alone product while Microsoft counters that the software is part of Windows 95, not a separate product. The courts had to decide if this prevented competition. They must ensure windows 95 and Internet Explorer can be placed on computers while at the same time stimulating competition.

In addition to these federal laws mentioned, many states have supplemented the laws with their own. For example, Florida has the Florida Antitrust Act of 1980, which is meant to complement the federal laws which I discussed in this chapter. All of this barely scratches the surface of some of the laws that affect contracts.

INTELLECTUAL PROPERTY

CHAPTER SEVEN

Three things compose intellectual property:

- Patents

- Trademarks

- Copyrights

Patents

Each is a type of property created by a person who can obtain exclusive rights to the "property" that was created. Patents are, by far, the most complex of the three. Patents provide protection from unauthorized duplication and/or use of unique inventions. For example, you create a new type of mechanical chair for people who cannot walk. Obviously, before you sell that chair you want some protection.   You need to ensure that no one can steal your invention, call it his/her own, and profit from your invention.

You want to make sure you "own" your invention. This will provide you with several rights. You will have the right to market your product free from interference, the right to be the exclusive seller of the product, or to allow only those people you approve of to sell your product. You also have the right to find suppliers to quote manufacture of your product without fear that the suppliers will take your idea and use it as their own.

These rights become yours when you get a patent for your invention. Several fairly simple steps must be completed to obtain a patent: complete and fill out the application (which includes a drawing of the invention, such as blueprints), mail in the fee, publish your invention and meet all the requirements to be entitled to a patent. Do note that a patent application most often requires some degree of specialization to complete.

Patent requirements included:

• Inventorship – the application must be filed by the inventor or inventors.

• Novelty – the invention must be new.

• Utility – the invention must be useful.

• Patentability – the subject matter must be patentable.

Inventorship raises several issues. Let's say you own a tire manufacturing company. The machine you currently use takes about an hour to mold one tire out of the rubber. Now, one of your employees says he thinks he can build a machine that will do it faster and asks to work on this project on company time. You say yes, and six months later this employee has invented a new machine that creates the tire in ten minutes. Seems great, right?

But, according to patent law the inventor must apply for the patent. The inventor therefore owns the tire machine, not you. You will need to negotiate with the employee for the right to use the machine that he invented on company time.

To protect yourself against this occurrence you need to have employees who perform services for your company, and have the potential to create a patentable invention, sign an employment agreement. This agreement would contain among other provisions a work for hire clause. For example:

"Any and all discoveries, inventions and/or creations by the Employee during the term of his employment shall become the property of the Employer. Employee hereby agrees that he shall execute any documents necessary to assign the rights for such intellectual property to the Employer at the request of Employer".

By signing an agreement with such a provision, the employee agrees that any of his inventions become the property of his employer. The employee executes an assignment of patents, and when the patent is issued it becomes the property of the company. Many companies do reward employees for a patented invention that provides benefits to the company. For example, a large jet engine manufacturer gives a $750 bonus to the employee responsible for the patent when the application is submitted, then another $250 and a plaque when the patent is approved. Such rewards, however, are nowhere near the total benefits the company receives as a result of the invention.

The concept of novelty also raises several issues. For example, what if you take something that has already been invented outside the United Sates and try to patent it here? What if you take an existing invention and change it slightly? What if you make a new invention and never get a patent for it – does this mean that no one can use the invention? These are some of the complex questions which surround patents. You need to recognize these issues and others that exist which can potentially create problems for your company. My best advice here would be to find an experienced patent attorney. These lawyers, who have passed a second bar, have the specialized expertise required to protect your company.

An invention must also be useful for something that is patentable. For example, you cannot patent an idea. Let's say you get an idea for a warp drive for rockets. That would be an important invention. It's a great idea. However, you cannot patent the concept of a warp drive. If you could, you could keep others from working on an invention just because you thought of the concept first. Instead, you must actually create the warp drive to be entitled to the patent.

Trademarks

Trademarks offer protection for a corporate identity. When you create a company you are going to choose a logo and a name for your company. Obviously, just as you patent an invention, you want to protect the logo and corporate name. Hence, you will apply for a trademark by filling out a relatively simple application.

To get a trademark you must:

- Have a trademark that is unique.

- Be the first to use that trademark in interstate commerce.

- Complete the application and approval process.

The trademark application and approval process can be very limiting when granting a trademark. When you fill out a trademark application you have to state the specific categories of business for which you are applying. For example, you are creating an airline called Skyview Airlines. You want to protect that name so no one else can use it. In the application you will most likely state that you want the trademark for advertisement and airline transportation purposes.

You must be very specific when indicating what classes you seek to protect. And if you do not choose the right classes, you do not get full protection.

With the application, you receive a list of categories and classes to choose from, and it is relatively simple to draft the application. In fact, the government employees are quite helpful during the application process. An application for a trademark, which is easier to fill out and requires considerably less than an application for a patent, can be completed by anyone.

Copyrights

The third type of intellectual property is a copyright. Copyright protection applies to works such as books. When you write a book you do not want anyone stealing part of the book and reprinting it without your permission. We therefore seek to have the work copyrighted. As with patents and trademarks, copyrights have a unique application process, which includes submitting the complete work.

It is important to note that several things are not copyrightable, including:

- Titles

- Names or Slogans

- Ideas

- Plans

- Blank Books Such as Diaries

- Works, which are common knowledge (for example, calendars).

Copyrights protect original works of authorship, such as:

Literature

Music

Drama

Motion Pictures

Architectural Works

Sculpture and Art

Choreography

The work for hire clause, which I mentioned previously, would also be used to assign any copyrights to the company. For example, should you write a book on company time, it becomes the company's property.

As I mentioned in the earlier discussion of confidentiality, you will need to provide for protection of your company's copyrights and any inventions, which may be developed as a result of this contractual relationship in your contracts as well.

No matter which type of intellectual property you decide to use, remember these important points:

- Provide for intellectual property in contracts.

- Deal with the issue of work for hire.

- Make sure your rights are protected.

Keep in mind, having ownership of intellectual property is good but you must go to the next step and zealously protect your property. This raises a whole new set of problems. Let's say you have a patent and discover someone using your patented invention without your permission. The patent enforcement process can be both lengthy and costly. The first step involves seeking an injunction. To get an injunction you must go to court and seek to stop another person from using the invention for which you hold the exclusive rights. If the court finds a violation of your patent rights, the court will issue an injunction, which legally prevents an infringer from continuing to use your invention. You may also be entitled to damages for the infringement if damages arose.

Think of the amount of time and money this will cost. It is of primary importance for any person or entity who owns intellectual property to diligently enforce his rights. That means anytime someone infringes your copyright you have to go after the person. If you do not, you will be giving up the protection you have received. You are in essence giving your invention or creation to the public. Of course, there are many defenses to claims of infringement. In the case of copyright infringement, such claims include independent creation and public knowledge of the information.

This covers the basics of intellectual property. My goal was not to explain all the ins and outs of patents, trademarks and copyrights. Instead, I hope you come away from this chapter with the knowledge that in any contract you may have there should be some consideration as to whether or not you need to provide for intellectual property rights, and if so, what form that coverage will take.

PROBLEMS IN CONTRACTS

CHAPTER EIGHT

When I began writing this book I tried to think of why people would pick up this book. Obviously, you are working somehow on contracts. You use contracts in your job or deal with them on a daily basis and would like to know more. Or, more likely, something isn't going right and you need to get a handle on problems that you face.

I asked people what problems they have experienced with contracts and used this chapter to address many of them. I have divided this chapter into sections so you can look at those sections which apply to you. However, be advised that you may not currently be involved in all of the problems I address here now, but most likely you will have all the problems at some point. So read them all and learn how to protect yourself.

You Know What You Want; Why Can't You Get It?

After reading this book you should have a pretty good idea of what you want in a contract. If you are like me you can even create a dream contract, which contains all of those perfect clauses that you want. Sometimes, though that doesn't do you any good.

Contracts are most often a function of your power as a negotiator. You cannot get what you want in a contract if you do not have the ability to negotiate for it. Let's say you are a buyer. You want warranties. You want the breach of warranty to be a material breach of the contract. You want substantial damages in the case of a breach. However, the seller uses a standard form contract.

You really need this item you want to purchase, but the seller says either sign the contract or don't buy the product. Some sellers don't care; numerous other companies will buy their products if you do not. What choice do you really have? Oddly enough, this situation is more common than negotiating. Since you cannot negotiate, you might believe that all of your training and knowledge of contracts will not help you in this case.

However, when a seller forces you to sign a standard form agreement, you can at least read and understand what you are signing.

In some cases the best solution may be to go somewhere else and not sign the agreement. Think about it. We are trying to build win/win relationships here. We are trying to establish a partnership. However, there is only one side willing to compromise. There is no easy solution to this problem. My best suggestion is to negotiate what you can and to at least put in a clause that will allow you to get out of the contract if you need to.

The Battle of the Forms

Most contracts are not drafted for a particular case. We have standard contracts, such as a purchase order, which we use all the time, and have been approved by our legal department. Standard contracts seem like a good thing.

We can rely on the contract because we have used it before and it has been approved by Legal. We also do not have to worry about trying to write a contract ourselves without having full knowledge of contracts. Lawyers have, in this case, drafted the contract for the company employees and taken it out of their hands. However, we can be hurt by standard form contracts as well. Every situation is different and a standard form contract may not adapt to those new situations.

The buyer has a standard form contract. The seller has a standard form contract as well. The buyer has a purchase order. The seller has a written confirmation for the buyer's purchase orders. Each of these contracts has different clauses and favors a different party, which only serves to compound the problems caused by inflexibility.

This is referred to as the battle of the forms, contracts with different and conflicting provisions going back and forth. Rather than go into a long legal description let me say that if you are not careful and a problem arises you are going to go to court over the contracts. The buyer will say the purchase order is the contract and the seller will say the written confirmation is the contract.

I don't care what the law says, a judge is going to determine the terms of the contract. Both sides are going to spend a lot of money on lawyers and what started out as a partnership is going to be destroyed. Therefore, you need to do something to protect yourself.

If you use a purchase order and you receive a written confirmation back, you should immediately send a letter to the other side stating that your purchase order is the controlling document. You should also reject the written confirmation and send it back to the other side.

The problem is compounded again if we have a blanket order agreement. Purchase orders are executed off the blanket purchase order. Add written confirmations and you can see the problem this creates. You have numerous agreements going back and forth, probably going to different people.

Remember the best place to start is the largest agreement. In this case, the basic order agreement is the controlling document. In your contract you should have a clause, which specifies how the agreement will work. We can state that purchase orders and written confirmations can both be issued with a basic order agreement in order to be effective. These other items should be considered part of the agreement. You should also place in the agreement a clause which states that if any terms or conditions conflict in the basic order agreement, the purchase order or the written confirmation, the terms of the basic order agreement shall control. This will protect you against conflicting terms and conditions in the battle of the forms.

How Many Contracts Can One Company Have?

I am amazed at how many different contracts a company uses in its day-to-day operations. Each contract is a unique entity, most likely drafted by a different individual in the company. As a purchasing professional, how do you know whether to use a standard form contract or to draft one for yourself?

That is a difficult question to answer. Most purchases tend to be run of the mill. When buying office supplies such as pencils and paper, the likely choice to use would seem to be a standard purchase order. On the other hand, maybe you are buying a large computer system. You have drafted a Request for Proposal and have received responses back. Let's further assume that you are going to spend several million dollars on this computer system. In this case, you would likely draft a contract specifically tailored to the situation.

The important thing for any company to do, especially one with a large purchasing department or several purchasing departments scattered across the globe, is to somehow coordinate the department activities. Some purchasing departments coordinate through their legal department. Others use computer systems that allow corporate purchasing professionals to share information with each other.

Computerized contract software is a powerful tool. Anyone in the company can look at any locations or person's contracts. Everyone knows whether a change has been made to a contract and can benefit from the knowledge. Also, company guidelines become immediately accessible. If someone makes an unauthorized change to a contract, it will not be approved or will be automatically forwarded for approval.

Making Sure You Cover Everything in a Contract

Drafting a contract, any contract, can be a scary experience, especially when you are trying to cover yourself for every conceivable possibility.

- What clauses do you use?

- How should the clauses be worded?

- How do you protect yourself?

The best answer to these questions is to hire a lawyer. But that isn't always the answer. Not every company has a legal department, and even if you have a legal department, how do you know when to use them? Plus, not every contract requires a lawyer. Finally, lawyers cost money. As a general rule, the bigger the contract the more likely you will need legal counsel.

My best suggestion is to make a list of contract clauses and pick and choose. In Chapter Eleven we will go over the various contract clauses. Use that as a start and decide what you need and do not need. Once you decide on the clauses you want to include, you can determine the precise wording of those clauses.

Your company may also have standard form contracts for you to use. Let me stress that experience is the best teacher. I always learn from my mistakes. No matter how long I work at contracts, and I do this for a living, I find that I still make mistakes. Something goes wrong and you think to yourself, I could have protected my client against this if only I had included certain clauses.

Believe me the next time you draft that contract you will make sure you include the clauses you previously left out. Experience really is the best teacher, and that is one of the best reasons for using experienced lawyers.

Involving People in Your Corporation

In Chapter Five we talked about the rules regarding agency. For now, let's just say that everyone in your company can bind your company by executing a contract on its behalf. Since that is true, you better make sure your company has clear internal procedures regarding contracts. Additionally, you need to make sure that you and anyone you work with are well trained.

You need to know:

- Whether standard contracts are used.

- When to use standard contracts and when to write your own.

- When to consult the legal department for approval.

- The limits of your authority and your coworkers' authority

Many companies have policy and procedure manuals which detail what employees must do in their jobs. Companies have also begun to employ the ever growing amount of contract software in the market which can help them create and share contracts and ideas internally.

A company should have a well-trained staff. This can mean seminars for key employees or books such as this one for employees to review and use in their jobs. It also means feedback. As I said before, people learn from mistakes. I teach people the mistakes I've made so they will not make the same ones. This same concept should also be applied internally. Employees should share with coworkers what they have experienced with suppliers so that others may benefit.

Companies must empower their people and enable them to do their jobs with knowledge and confidence. That means educating them about contracts. It also means educating them about lawyers.

Dealing With the Legal Department

A major problem in the contracting process can arise from trying to deal with a legal department, either internal or external. Lawyers serve an important purpose. Sure, we all know the lawyer jokes.

What do you call 1000 lawyers at the bottom of the ocean? A good start.

Why didn't the snake kill the lawyer? Professional courtesy.

Lawyers are put down in our society, sometimes with good reason. But, they are important to the contract process. Most purchasing professionals do not know the law. They know their business. The lawyers are there to fill in the blanks. It is up to the clients to inform the lawyers as carefully as possible about what they do or do not need.

A lawyer must be managed by his client. A lawyer can suggest 100 things to go into a perfect contract, but it is up to the client to give the lawyer guidance about what the contract needs. A lawyer does not know your business. You are the best judge of what you need your contract to protect you against. The lawyer can draft the language that will protect you. You and your lawyer have to work together on the contract.

But, remember one important detail: You will be the one signing the contract. It is your butt on the line. If you cannot live with the contract you need to change it. Never, ever, sign a contract you do not agree with.

Okay, So Your Contract Is Great. What Good Does That Do You?

Hopefully, this book will lay the groundwork for you to draft, or work with your attorney to draft, an ideal contract. But, what if you cannot negotiate a good contract? Or, even worse, what if you negotiate and sign a contract then learn you have forgotten something?

Contracts are funny things. Sometimes airtight contracts are not the great things you think they are. I negotiated a great contract for one of my clients. He had been burned by this supplier in the past. The supplier had previously backed out of a contract, so my client wanted to protect himself from the same thing happening again. The current contract protected him against that occurrence by imposing penalties if either party backed out of the contract early.

Sounds great, and my client should have been happy. But, as often happens, the unforeseen occurred. My client found a much better deal somewhere else and was the one who wanted to get out of the contract. The airtight contract ended up hurting my client since his company had to stay with the deal when he wished to change to another supplier. The moral of the story, be careful what you wish for because you just might get it.

So what happens when you feel you need to breach a contract and don't really know how to get out of it? Depending on the situation, you might just want to breach the contract and live with the consequences. I've had clients who have done just that.

I just talked about my client who could have saved so much money by going with another supplier. He decided he would use the other supplier and live with the consequences. When the first supplier threatened to sue, we negotiated the best deal possible to get my client out of the contract.

Contracts as Living Documents

Another problem arises when you have a contract and something goes wrong. We are going to talk about remedies in the next chapter. But, what good do remedies do when your contract is going south. Contracts are based on partnerships and any time a contract goes bad so does the partnership. If you have a contract that someone is breaching, that agreement is not worth the paper it is written on.

The whole basis for contracts is a moral responsibility and an effort to make a relationship between two people that can be relied upon in the long term. If you have to rely on suing for remedies it will cost time and money. Really, you are worse off than when you started. The partnership is more important than the contract. If you are forcing the other side to sign a contract, you are going to be in trouble at some point. The other side certainly feels no obligation to do right by you if you need help.

In a partnership the contract is just the start of the relationship. I tell my clients that contracts are living documents that are never cast in stone. The parties should always be open to changes. If one side is having a problem with the contract, it should be able to go to the other side and discuss the problem. At this point, both sides should try to renegotiate the terms of the contract to suit both sides, a win/win outcome. That is what a partnership is about.

REMEDIES FOR BREACH OF AGREEMENT

CHAPTER NINE

Previously we talked about the three types of breaches of agreement and how it was up to you to classify the breach in your agreement. Our next step is to determine what the remedy will be when one party breaches the agreement. "Remedies" is a broad term meant to cover all types of recovery that you can get when you sue someone and win. It's not enough to just sue the other side; you have to ask the court for some type of recovery.

Remedies are generally divided as follows:

Seller's Remedies:

- Withhold delivery of the goods

- Stop delivery by carrier

- Resell the goods and recover the difference

- Cancel

- Damages

Buyer's Remedies:

- Cancel

- Cover

- Recover goods identified to the contract

- Specific performance

- Damages

Damages

In general, damages, the most common type of remedy, are what you want to get in the event of a breach. That sounds easy, but as with any element of a contract, the hardest part is deciding what you want before you really know. Lawyers get paid to tell clients all the things that can go wrong, but they rely on the client to voice their needs. It is very difficult to know what you want because when you write a contract you do not want to think about something going wrong. However, you have to carefully prepare for a breach. Assume it will happen...now what are you going to do? Be careful, in order to be entitled to damages, you must provide for them in your contract.

Damages are probably the easiest remedy to explain. Damages can generally be defined as compensation for injury. As a rule, in damages we want to put the person who was injured in the same place he would be if the contract had been performed in full. The wronged party does have a duty to mitigate its damages. If a buyer is damaged because parts were not received, it is the buyer's duty to find the parts somewhere else in order to lessen the amount of damages which will be claimed.

The buyer cannot wait and let damages accumulate. If there is something that he can do to stop the damages from increasing, there is a duty to take that action. Otherwise, damages will not be recoverable. This duty does not require success in mitigating damages, only that an attempt to lessen the damages be made.

Punitive Damages

There are also punitive damages, which are extra damages we charge against a party because of bad or malicious conduct. Awarding the party punitive damages helps to deter other people from doing the same thing. In essence, we are making an example of the breaching party. Even though very large punitive damage awards make headlines, punitive damages are a highly unusual remedy and are increasingly difficult to obtain.

Liquidated damages, is a type of punitive damage which, are specified in a contract as a way to deter the other party from breaching the contract. To do this we put an incremental amount of damages in the contract, which the parties agree will be proper in the event of a breach. Again, there will need to be proof that these liquidated damages are not a penalty. They must have some basis in fact. You will also not be able to get liquidated damages if damages could have been calculated easily. The lesson to be learned here is that if you are going to put liquidated damages in a contract, make sure that the amount has some relation to actual damages and make sure that they are clearly spelled out. The damages should not be open to interpretation.

Other Types of Damages

Compensatory Damages:

Specifically compensatory damages seek to put the harmed party in the same financial position they would have been had the contract been performed. Generally, this means awarding the wronged party the amount of profit they would have received under the contract.

Restitution:

Damages for restitution are awarded against a person who has been unjustly enriched. The party who has been unjustly enriched is required to make restitution to the wronged party by compensating them. The basic premise of restitution is to put the wronged party in the same place he has before the contract was made. In other words, we want to make the plaintiff whole. You cannot, generally, get both restitution and other damages. You cannot be "made whole" and receive additional damages.

Specific Performance:

A plaintiff also has the choice to obtain the remedy of specific performance. Specific performance is really a simple concept. It means that you want to get the defendant to do exactly what he promised to do in the contract. The most common example of a case where you want to get specific performance is a real estate contract. If the seller breaches the contract, the buyer may want to go to court to enforce the contract and compel the sale of the home pursuant to the terms of the agreement. Specific performance is another difficult remedy to obtain. The primary reason for this difficulty is the fact that legal remedies must be inadequate for the court to compel this remedy. To get specific performance, damages cannot make you whole. Using the house example, you want the house, not the money.

Injunction:

The remedy of an injunction is also a type of specific performance remedy. An injunction is a ruling by the court that stops a person from performing some activity that is in breach of the contract. In other words, you are specifically enforcing the contract provisions. However, an injunction is a difficult remedy to obtain. To begin with, to obtain an injunction you are faced with the difficult task of proving that damages are inadequate. And again, you must have reserved the right to get an injunction in the agreement.

Let me give you an example of what I mean by "inadequate". Let's say you own a business and an employee leaves to start his own business and one of your major clients follows the employee. You feel the employee stole your client. If this person continues to work with the client, how much do you stand to lose over the next two years? That is the future. There is no way of telling exactly how much revenue that client could have generated for you. Consequently, you seek an injunction to stop the former employee. That way there will be no damages for the two years.

Right to Cancel:

If someone breaches a contract one of the remedies you can obtain is the right to cancel. The right to cancel lets you get out of the contract actions that you would otherwise be obligated to perform. You would legally get out of the contract and, as a result, not be obligated to pay the other party damages for not performing.

Termination for Convenience:

Many parties put a clause in their contracts called "termination for convenience", which allows a party to cancel the contract for any reason whatsoever. It usually contains a sentence, which says you have to give so many days' notice to the other party prior to cancellation, usually 30 days. My best piece of advice, do not make this mutual. Why would you let the supplier out of the contract after taking so much time to negotiate it?

Termination for Cause:

Some contracts contain a termination clause that only allows termination for cause. You can only cancel this type of contract upon the occurrence of certain events. Events you have specified exactly. One condition for termination often found in this clause is a breach by either party. That sounds simple, but you may have to go to court to prove the other side breached the contract.

I want to reiterate the fact that you must specify in the contract what you consider a breach. I often tell my clients, "If you want something to be a breach of the contract, we need to state in the document what the event is, as specifically as possible". Since you probably can't think of everything, you'll want to include what I call "magic words". The phrase "including but not limited to" basically says, "Here are all the things I can think of, and if I forgot anything, I'm including them too".

Remedy of Cover:

The remedy of cover gives the wronged party the right to seek similar goods elsewhere. If your goods are not delivered on time that obviously can create several problems, especially if your shop functions in a just-in-time environment where you do not have a warehouse which stores safety stock for your assembly line. The right to cover allows you to get similar goods from another source. If there is an increased price because you are going to another source you would seek to recover that loss, as damages, from the breaching party. As you can see, you want to carefully set out the damages as well as your right to cover in the contract.

Resale of Goods:

The other side of covering is reselling the goods. If you are the seller and the buyer fails to go through with the purchase of the goods, the seller has the right to find another party to buy the goods and to sue for damages. In that case, the damages would be the difference in the profit he would have received for the goods. If you sell the goods to a third party for more than the price negotiated with the breaching party, be prepared to have that difference credited to the breaching party and subtracted from any damages awarded to you.

Recovery of Goods:

Sometimes parties want to recover their goods, in particular goods identified in the contract. Let's assume goods, such as computer housings, have been produced for you. You have paid for the goods, and the goods even have your name on them. However, they sit in the seller's warehouse waiting for delivery. Now, the seller has breached the contract. One of the things you want is to retrieve those goods from the seller's location. It's easy to identify your products because they are clearly marked. Obviously, you will need to provide for this in your contract and clearly state how and when you can get the goods sent to you.

Delay or Stop Delivery:

The seller, on the other hand, may want to either delay delivery or stop delivery altogether in the event of a breach by the buyer. If the two parties have an installment contract where the buyer is going to purchase 100 widgets a month for ten months and the buyer has not paid for the last three deliveries, the seller is certainly going to want to delay the next delivery until he received payment for the last few shipments. You need to reserve this right in your contract or you are obligated to continue to make deliveries even though you are not getting paid for the previous ones.

Hold in Escrow:

Related to the recovery of goods, is holding some item in escrow to be released upon the occurrence of certain events. For example, many times companies have computer programs created specifically for their use. Those programs have source code, the computer language that runs the program. If something goes wrong, the user will need to get to that source code to use it or modify it. Escrow agents, who are independent of the two parties in the contract, are people who hold source code or other items and agree to release that code upon any number of occurrences, such as a breach. You will need to have a contract with the escrow agent that states when you want to give out the source code. If either party thinks there is a breach, he can make a claim to the escrow agent, who can either make a decision or wait while a lawsuit is filed. Escrow is difficult to get and one should be careful before using this remedy.

As a general rule, by using damages of any kind you seek to put the harmed party in the same place it would be if the breach had not taken place. Again, you must go to court to prove damages. For example, if you seek damages against an ex-employee who went to work for a competitor, taking one of your clients with him, you will have to prove what that client was worth to you. You may also be entitled to damages, which include interest and attorney fees.

Attorney's Fees:

Usually, when you sue for damages you do not get attorney's fees. That means you can spend ten thousand dollars in legal fees to collect $2000 and have no recovery. There are three exceptions to this case. First, you can be entitled to attorney's fees when they are provided for by statute. Second, attorney's fees can be obtained when you reserve the right for attorney's fees in your contract. This is very close to the concept of incidental damages. Finally, you can get attorney's fees if a judge awards them. However, without a statutory or contract provision, this would be a highly unusual remedy. I find this remedy to be very underutilized by purchasers.

All of these remedies do not include damages, which can be granted to third party beneficiaries to the contract. A third party may be entitled to any of the damages, which I listed previously. Of course, the third party will need to be made a party to the law suit. Additionally, it must be proven that the third party was in privity to the contract. That means that the third party must be a foreseeable party in the contract such that any defendant would know that he could owe some other person or entity damage for any breach.

Defenses against Damage Claims

Right to Cure:

There are also defenses to any claim for damages. First of all, the defendant should be given a chance to correct any breach. This is called the right to cure. Let's say you received your order for a set of parts. Generally, you are going to inspect those parts before you send them to the assembly line. What if the parts are bad? You intend to return the parts and either get a credit and buy the goods somewhere else, or you want to exchange the parts. You should give the seller the right to take the nonconforming goods back and to give you conforming parts in their place.

Proof of Damages:

Of course, as with any other element of a contract, cost, profit, quality, time and the like, will all have to be set out, as evidence, for the judge or jury. So, even if you think the chances of a breach are slim, you still need to carefully document everything related to the contract.

Limits on Recovery:

A court may limit your recovery in any case. You may only get what expenses you incurred and may not be given profit. Your damages may only be the present value of the damages as determined by the court. Or damages may be reduced for many other reasons. I have seen the best contracts go down in flames in front of a judge or jury. Having the most airtight contract in existence does not ensure that the other party will not breach the contract. And if that contract is breached the court may not award the damages you asked for in the contact.

Being awarded damages you asked for does not guarantee you will collect a single penny. I had a client win $600,000 after two years of lawsuits and headaches only to have the defendant go bankrupt. All that time and effort for no return. Even worse, my client still had his legal bills to deal with.

When I look at contracts I usually see poorly drafted damage provisions. Generally, when we enter into contacts we only think of the performance of the good things in the contract. We rarely deal with what will happen if something goes wrong. I cannot stress enough how important it is to determine the following things:

- When you want damages.

- What damages will be available to you; and

- The amount of method of calculation for any liquidated damages.

In conclusion, carefully set out what damages you want and then make sure you keep careful records in the ordinary course of your business so that if you ever need to prove your damages, you can have the information at your fingertips.

CONTRACT ADMINISTRATION & MANAGEMENT

CHAPTER TEN

Let's assume you have a contract, which you are happy with at the time you sign it. This chapter deals with many of those other elements of working with contracts and other companies in the uncertain world we live in. All too often we execute contracts and forget that these are documents we will have to live with for many years to come.

I break contracts into three phases:

1. Negotiations

2. Contract

3. Contract Administration and Management

Back in Chapter One we discussed the three phases. Chapter Three dealt with negotiations and their importance. Chapter Four, Nine and Eleven discuss the contract phase. In the real world, Phase One and Phase Two take up relatively little time in relation to the contract as a whole. Do not forget that contracts are living, breathing documents. They should adapt to new and unforeseen situations.

That means you do not just put the contract in a drawer once it is signed and forget about it. There are provisions that should survive the termination of the contract, and there are duties you need to be aware of that may come back to hurt you if you are not prepared for them.

Remember my client who leased the building? I told you about how she did not consider the fact that the price of the lease would increase each year based on the consumer price index. Taking my lead from her I had negotiated the important provisions to her satisfaction and gave her the contract to review. As I said, when the rent went up, we called the landlord and renegotiated the escalation clause so that it was removed from the contract in the second year.

My biggest mistake was making two assumptions. First, I assumed she would read and understand the contract. Second, I figured if she had any problems with other provisions of the contract that she would tell me about them, and we would discuss the problems. Several lessons can be learned from this.

Your legal department is only as good as you are. In some cases, when you sit down with your lawyer, you actually know more about the law of purchasing than they do. Just because they are a lawyer does not make them knowledgeable about contracts.

My client thought I was taking care of everything. But as a rule, clients do not want to pay a lot of money for legal services. So, what should you as a purchasing professional do? Do you take the time to go over every paragraph of the contract with your lawyer so that you know everything? Or, do you read the contract and go to the lawyer with any questions you may have? I suppose the answer is somewhere in between the two choices.

This is really about contract ownership. Someone has to own the contract. Someone has to be responsible for this document. Someone needs to ensure that all the responsibilities of both parties are completed. We will talk more about this later.

In general, my clients are the owners of the contracts. They have to live with them. It belongs to them. As a lawyer I can advise but it's not my decision whether or not to sign the contract. The ultimate decision making rests with my clients. I can't tell you how many times I advised my clients against doing something only to have them do it anyway. In this case, my client who was signing the contract had better read it and understand what she is reading. If she does not understand something, or if she has a problem with any element of the contract, I am available to help.

It is your duty as a client to inform your attorney of your expectations regarding the contract. Do you want him to protect you against certain things? Are there portions of the contract you don't understand? Are there things you need to ensure are in the contract? As the owner of the contract, it is your job to make sure you understand and accept every provision of the contract. Just because your legal department approves the contract does not mean you should sign the contract without reading it so you know what you are obligated to do.

Remember: Your lawyer may know the law, but may not know your business. That is why you are there. The lessons to be learned are to make sure you communicate with your lawyer and to make sure you do your job: read and understand the document.

Hey, you can't do that!

This part of the lesson comes under the heading of the most well prepared people, who have the best contracts, have often gone to court regardless of what the contract states. I am constantly asked in class how to stop someone from breaching a contract. The simple answer to that question is you don't. I don't care how great your contract is, you can never stop someone from breaching the contract, if that is what they want to do. In fact, I have clients who come to me and say, "We want to breach this contract; what is our liability"?

So since you can't stop someone from breaching the contract, what are you as a purchasing professional, to do? Here are some suggestions:

- Never let the other side off the hook.

- Develop a reputation.

- Have very good contracts.

- Address any problems immediately.

As I stated before, contracts are living documents. Because contracts are living documents, you may have cases where a minor breach of the contract is committed. Since it is a minor breach, you may choose to do nothing about the breach. However, you need to make sure that you do some simple things to protect yourself and your company. First, regardless of the type of breach, if the other party breaches the contract, notify them, in writing, of that fact. This does not mean you have to do anything further about the breach. The letter shows you are aware of the breach and are not turning a blind eye.

You should also include a clause in your contracts, which says, in part: "For any breach, any inaction by the non-breaching party shall not operate as a waiver for any subsequent breach". In English, this means that not doing anything about a breach which occurs now does not mean that you cannot do something about a future breach. This is important. Often times if you do not do anything about a breach, even a minor one, you waive your rights to do something about the breach next time.

This situation is commonly found in employment contracts. Many contracts contain non-compete clauses, which state that an employee cannot compete against the corporation after leaving its employ. There are several reasons for this: your employee had no prior experience, you provided the employee significant training or your employee has learned many trade secrets he or she can use against your company.

Let's assume your employee has signed a contract with a non-compete clause. This employee then leaves your company and breaches his or her contract by competing with your company in direct violation of the contract. Let's also assume that you do nothing about it. Either the employee is not actually hurting the company or you cannot afford legal action or you don't think you can win. By doing nothing, you are waiving your rights to sue for future breaches, as I will explain.

This is one of many instances involving contracts where you need to sue so that you do not waive your rights at a later date. In the field of non-compete law, if you do not go after the wrongdoer the first time someone breaches a non-compete clause in a contract, you cannot sue the next time someone else breaches the contract. There is a reason for this harsh rule. If you do not pursue the first person you are giving the impression to the other employees in your company that you are not going to enforce that provision of the contract. Because of the implied view you are giving your other employees, they are more likely to compete with you when they leave, because they think it is all right. The law holds it against you if you give people that impression.

The lesson to be learned here is to make sure you actively pursue employees who breach contracts. That does not mean you have to sue every time. You can send a letter. You can negotiate a settlement. You can amend the contact. Just do something to send a message that you are not going to be taken advantage of.

That leads to the second point. You must develop a reputation as a company that actively enforces its contracts. The company I used to work for had many contracts with independent contractors. Because the contractors used this company's materials there was a risk that the contractors would take the materials and use them as their own.

To minimize this threat, I advised my client to develop a reputation for being tough on offenders. When the first person broke the contract and used my client's materials as his own we immediately did something about it. We attempted to negotiate a settlement. When that failed, we sued. We also made sure that everyone in the company knew this was going on. We wanted to send a message; "Don't breach your contract with us, or we will take legal action".

In sum you should actively protect your company in contracts, but at the same time you should be fair in the process. One way to be fair is to have excellent contracts. I often teach at companies and have a chance to look at many different types of contracts. More often than not, a purchasing contract takes the form of a blanket agreement with purchase orders operating as releases against that agreement. Each of these agreements have various terms and conditions, some of which may conflict with one another. You will need to make sure as the owner of your contract that the terms in the various contracts do not conflict with each other. That means clearly spelling out which documents will govern in what circumstances.

Also, remember these documents are most likely standard

form agreements. The difficulty in standard form agreements is their inability to adapt to every situation. There is something unusual about every situation, something that makes it unique. Your contract should adapt. However, that is often not the case. Having one contract makes it easier. Legal has already reviewed the contract. You know it works because you have used it before. But, you need to have a way to change the contract to meet the needs of the unique situations that will come up. Terms will change. Clauses some companies will agree to may be more difficult for other companies to agree to. You need to supervise all of this. And it is also up to you to make sure the other side understands the contract it is signing.

This is increasingly difficult when you have subcontractors in other countries. They may speak a different language or their understanding of some terms may be different from yours. Make sure your contract has a definition section. This section spells out the meaning of the essential terms in the contract: How do you define a material breach? What is on-time delivery?

Also make sure you are included under the notice section of the contract. The notice section tells you where any notices under the contract should be sent. Putting your name there ensures you will always be kept up to date and included in any communications regarding the contract.

The last point is to address any problems immediately, which should be obvious by now. Do not wait. If you know something is happening that needs your attention do not delay. I see it all the time; one side breaches the contract, and my client does not want to say anything about it. They have more deliveries under contract and do not want to hurt the deliveries. They have more pressing matters, better things to do with their time. But, as soon as you are aware of a problem, address the issue with the other side. Maybe you are the one who might breach the contract. You are the shipper, and you think the product might be delayed. But, you do not want to say anything because you really hope the delivery will make it in time.

Saying something at the earliest possible moment does several things. First, it gets rid of the element of surprise. The other side cannot be caught off guard with a late delivery. Second, early notification lessens your chances for liability. The other side can mitigate its damages if it knows of a problem early enough. Finally, it helps the relationship because both sides are communicating. Communication is the foundation of any relationship.

It's not my problem.

I always find people passing the buck. "Oh, John is responsible for that" or "I didn't know I was supposed to do that" or "I didn't have time" "we forgot" "We were too busy". It seems many of us have forgotten what our jobs are, and we don't take responsibility for owning the contract.

I see it all the time: one person negotiates the contract, one person signs the contract and one person administers the contract. That is confusing. Who owns the contract then? The answer is all of them. Each person is responsible for making that contract work. All of you have to protect the company and notify the company of any problems that occur in the contract. Additionally, your lawyer or legal department holds some responsibility for the contract. But, as I said, they rely on you for information so that they can do their job better.

CONTRACT CLAUSES FOR YOU TO USE

CHAPTER ELEVEN

So, here is where you get your money's worth. I'm going to give you some contract clauses to get you started. I cringe at the thought of it. So, first a warning:

PLEASE! PLEASE! PLEASE!

DO NOT JUST USE WHAT I GIVE YOU IN THIS CHAPTER AND THINK YOUR PROBLEMS ARE SOLVED

Now, an explanation:

The clauses here are meant to get you started. Every situation is different. Consequently, the clauses I present in this book may be the exact opposite of what you need. Also, there are always two sides to every contract. Each side, most likely, wants something different. Therefore, it is safe to assume that even if what is in this chapter is good for one person it might be bad for another. With that in mind, use these clauses and their explanations to help you start.

I want to teach you that contracts flow, from one clause to the other. When you think of one clause it should immediately lead to other clauses. I want you to develop a checklist, and a way of thinking about contracts. Let's look at some examples.

Price

Remember you do not need to have a price in your contract according to the UCC. But you should at least have some way to determine the price.

Here is an example of how to state price in a contract if you are not sure what it will be:

Purchase Price: The purchase price hereunder shall be based upon a

valuation of the COMPANY to be established each year at the annual meeting of the MEMBERS, which meeting is generally held in January ("Annual Valuation").

If the contract is for several years you may want a price increase clause so that each year you will get more money for your goods. For Example:

Promptly after the end of the first lease year and at the end of each lease year thereafter, the Rental shall be adjusted by adding to the annual Base Rental the amount computed by multiplying the annual Base Rental by the fraction which has a numerator of the most recent Comparison Price Index minus the Base Price Index, and has a denominator of Base Price Index.

Quality

Quality is often determined by using specifications or other exhibits in your contract. You will note in this chapter that one paragraph leads to others and that your contract will grow through these related provisions. Here is how you should logically consider quality:

Quality leads to Exhibits leads to Inspection

Inspection leads to Breach leads to Remedies

Once you determine what standard of quality the goods must meet, you will need to illustrate this through exhibits. Carefully mark your exhibits and put their location in the contract if they cannot be attached. You will also have to determine how the goods will be inspected and what will constitute a failure of the goods. Also, state how many you will check. 100%? 10%? Once you determine when goods fail, you will state if it is a minor or material breach and determine the remedy.

Inspection: Buyer shall, in its sole discretion, inspect the goods to determine if the goods conform to the specifications as listed in the attached Exhibits to this Agreement. If 1% of goods received and inspected are determined by the Buyer, in its sole discretion, to be nonconforming, the entire shipment shall be determined to be nonconforming. Any nonconforming shipment shall be determined to be a material breach of this Agreement and the Buyer shall be entitled to any remedy allowed under this Agreement or by law.

Remedy

As you can see, the provision can get very tough. You will next have to determine what remedy you wish to receive. These can be any of the remedies, which we discussed previously. Next, I give you an example of a remedy provision giving the buyer the right to cover.

The object is to give yourself the broadest possible remedies from which to choose. You will also see how the contract logically flows from one provision to the other. The seller knows exactly what a breach of the contract is and what the consequences of that breach can be. Be aware of the fact that the provisions here are very simplified for the purpose of explanation and illustration. These paragraphs can actually go on for several pages by the time you add all the language. Remember my purpose here is to introduce you to the basics of contracts and how the paragraphs flow one to the other.

Remedy: Buyer, in the event of a material breach of this Agreement, as defined elsewhere in this Agreement, shall have the right, in the Buyer's sole discretion, to do any of the following:

Return nonconforming goods and seek a refund or credit for those goods, which have been returned.

Purchase like goods from another source. If the Buyer chooses this remedy, the Seller shall be responsible for the difference in any costs associated with such purchase; or Terminate this Agreement.

Indemnification

Indemnification provisions relieve one party from liability when the other party commits some wrongdoing and is sued by a third party. Here is a sample clause:

Indemnification: Agent will indemnify and hold harmless Company, and its successors and assigns, against any and all loss, injury, liability, claim, damage or expense (including without limitation, reasonable attorney's fees), interest, court costs and amounts paid in settlement of claims, suffered by Company, or its successors or assigns, resulting from any breach or failure to perform by Agent of any of its obligations under this Agreement and any inaccuracy in or breach of any of the representations, warranties, covenants or agreements made by Agent herein.

This paragraph will also be important when we talk about whether or not the parties to the contract are deemed to be partners. Indemnification usually requires that the party who is doing the indemnifying carry insurance at such an amount to cover what you want to be indemnified for. This clause is commonly found in contracts with construction companies.

Time

Contractor's agreements require a "time is of the essence" clause. This clause ensures that any delays are counted against the party who is on a deadline.

Insurance: Contractor shall purchase and maintain such insurance as will protect it from claims which may arise out of, or as a result from Contractor's operations under this Agreement, whether such operations be by itself or by any subcontractor or anyone directly or indirectly employed by any of them. This insurance shall be written for not less than any limits of liability specified, or required by law. Whichever is greater, and which shall include contractual liability insurance as applicable to Contractor's obligations or provided herein. Contractor will provide evidence of insurance at the request or Owner within three days of such request. Failure to obtain or provide evidence of such insurance shall be a material breach of this agreement.

Time is of the essence: Time is of the essence in this Agreement.

Arbitration: All disputes hereunder shall be resolved by binding arbitration in accordance with rules of the American Arbitration Association. The

Arbitration seems to be a very popular element of contracts.

I used to love arbitration provisions and put them in all my contracts. They are especially popular in agreements with contractors. However, once I used the provision I found I didn't like it as much as I thought I did. I had a dispute with a contractor, and we went to arbitration as required by the contract. We chose an arbitrator from a list. Neither of us had ever used the arbitrator we chose, though from what I had heard this man had a very good reputation.

When the day of the arbitration came we went to the offices of the court reporter. It was a nice place: a glass enclosed conference room overlooking the water. The other side arrived first and chose to sit with a view of the water. My client and I sat facing the reception area. I knew I was in even bigger trouble when the arbitrator walked right into the glass door of the conference room and knocked himself out. Needless to say, we lost the arbitration.

Arbitrators do not have to follow law; they can decide whatever they want. So before you choose arbitration, be warned. Although it is much less expensive and time consuming than court, it has its own unique set of drawbacks.

You will also notice the arbitration paragraph provides for attorney's fees. Again, this is a provision that may backfire. If you win, you win big. If you lose, you lose big. There also can be some dispute over who is a prevailing party in any suit. You can win some parts of the lawsuit and lose others.   Then it will be up to a court to determine which side, if any, is entitled to attorney's fees.

Termination

The following is a termination provision for a contract:

Termination: It is mutually agreed that either party may terminate this Agreement at the end of the Initial Term by giving the other party written notice thereof at least three (3) months prior to the end of the Initial Term. Should either party fail to give such notice, this Agreement shall continue upon the same terms and conditions in force immediately prior to the expiration of the Initial Term, for an additional period of one (1) year. After the Initial Term, either party may terminate the renewal of the Agreement by giving three (3) months written notice of its intention to terminate at any time prior to the expiration of the current term.

In this case, you would have to define how long the "Initial Term" of the Agreement is, usually one year.

Notice

From the termination clause, the next logical question is, where and how do I notify the other party? So, termination naturally flows into a notice provision.

Notice: Any notices under this Agreement may be sent by either certified mail, return receipt requested, or fax to the following people at the addresses listed below:

If to Seller: (name and address)

If to Buyer: (name and address)

You will use the notice provision for such items as notifications that the other party is in breach of the agreement, changes of address, changes to the contract and formal correspondence.

Non-partnership

Here is a provision that ensures two parties who enter into an agreement are not deemed to be partners:

This example, taken from a License Agreement, is linked to the paragraph where we talk about indemnity. Here we split the parties so that they are not partners. We then use an indemnity clause to relieve ourselves of liability in case the other party does something wrong. You do not want to have to watch the other side at all times, so you will need to relieve yourself of liability for anything the other side does. If someone sues the other party, you do not want to be sued as well. This clause will ensure the other side is independent:

No Partnership Created: The parties are independent contractors and nothing contained in this Agreement shall be deemed or interpreted to constitute the Licensee to be the agent or legal representative of Licensor for any purpose whatsoever. Licensee and licensor shall not be considered partners for any reason.

Entire Agreement

Entire Agreement clauses take into account the fact that while the parties may talk about things, unless they put any item in writing and sign the writing it does not become part of the contract. So, any verbal claims made by sales people have no bearing on the Agreement.

Entire Agreement Clause: This Agreement is the complete Agreement between the Company and the Agent and may be modified only by a written instrument executed by both the Company and Agent. This Agreement supersedes and renders void any prior agreement between the Company and the Agent. Please note here that this clause would render void any prior executed Confidentiality Agreement.

This is another example of how a contract logically flows from one clause to the other.

Merger Leads to Warranties Leads to Breach Clauses Leads to Remedies

Delivery

The following clause specifies the time, place and method of delivery. You will also see on the next page how delivery leads to other clauses as well.

Delivery: The widgets shall be delivered to the Buyer's place of business every Friday before 3 p.m. e.s.t. Widgets shall be shipped by carrier of Seller's choosing. Seller shall bear all risk of loss for the goods until such time as they reach Buyer's place of business. Seller shall carry sufficient insurance to protect itself against risk of loss and shall present evidence of such insurance at Buyer's request.

You will notice that I have left the concept of F.O.B. out of this example. The reason it is missing is I am a firm believer that you should spell out risk of loss in the contract. What if someone does not know what F.O.B. means? What if you are dealing with someone in a foreign country? If you do want to include the term in your contract, define it in the contract's definition section.

Delivery leads to Shipping Method leads to Risk of Loss Leads to Insurance leads to Indemnity

Warranties

If you put an entire agreement clause in your agreement you are, most likely, going to want to disclaim all warranties, since you do not want to be responsible for claims made by your sales person. The two clauses protect you. You should note that this will favor the Seller, not the Buyer.

DISCLAIMER OF WARRANTIES: SELLER DISCLAIMS ALL WARRANTIES EXPRESS AND IMPLIED, INCLUDING, BUT NOT LIMITED TO, THE IMPLIED WARRANTIES OF FITNESS FOR A PARTICULAR PURPOSE, USAGE OF THE TRADE AND MERCHANTABILITY.

As you can see, the disclaimer is in capital letters and bold print. This is one of the requirements for disclaiming warranties. This disclaimer must be conspicuous so that it catches the reader's eye. The buyer is giving up rights under this clause, and if there was a sales person making promises it takes on even more importance.

Also, you will see in this clause that I used the magic language "including but not limited to...." In contracts, that phase is very important. It refers to lists of items in contracts. For example, you want to list all the ways you can breach a contract. Obviously, you want to put as many things as possible in the list but, you cannot think of everything. You also want to ensure that if something comes up that you did not think of, it will also be included in the list. You use the phrase "including but not limited to" to list the items you can think of with the rest included by reference. An example, of a warranty is shown on the next page.

As you will see, the Representations and Warranties clause comes from a contract for hiring an agent. We want the agent to warrant several things: that he has the authority to enter into the Agreement and that the agreement has been approved by any corporate or governmental authorities that need to approve such an agreement.

Non-compete

Covenants not to compete are very popular in employment agreements these days. In essence, we are seeking to protect our business by ensuring that the employee does not take our clients. Be careful. These types of clauses are not accepted in EVERY state. Florida allows the clause. If you do use the clause it must be reasonable in the geographic scope, period of time and type of business you are limiting the employee from competing in.

Representations and Warranties:

(a) Agent has the full power and authority, without the consent of any person, to (i) execute and deliver this Agreement and to carry out the transactions contemplated hereby and (ii) own and operate its assets, properties and business.

(b) The execution, delivery and performance of this Agreement and the consummation of the transactions contemplated hereby have been duly and validly authorized by all necessary corporate action and when executed, this Agreement will be the valid and binding Agreement of Agent, enforceable

against Agent in accordance with its terms.

(c) Neither the execution or performance by Agent of this Agreement nor the compliance by Agent with the terms and provisions hereof, (i) will contravene any provision of any law, statute, rule or regulation or instrumentality or (ii) will conflict or be inconsistent with or result in a breach of any of the terms, covenants, conditions or provisions of, or constitute a default under the terms of any agreement, contract or instrument to which Agent is a party or by which any Agent's property or assets is bound or to which Agent may be subject.

Covenant not to compete:

Employee agrees that, during the term of employment hereunder and for a period of two (2) years after termination of employment, no matter how occasioned, he will refrain, directly or indirectly, from engaging in a business competitive with the company, whether alone as a partner or as an officer, director, employee or shareholder of any other corporation or as a trustee, fiduciary, or other representative of any other activity in the United States. Employee agrees that the area covered by this covenant not to compete is the United States in recognition that the company performs services in most states in the United States. This provision shall survive the termination of this Agreement.

Again, you will have to determine what the damages will be for a breach of this paragraph. One remedy you will definitely want to reserve for yourself is an injunction so that you can immediately stop the employee from working if he/she violates the non-compete paragraph.

Notice also that this paragraph survives the termination of the agreement. You need to expressly state that in your contract, or the other side can claim they thought the clause expired when the employee left the company. Do NOT leave any room for misunderstanding.

Covenants not to compete are unique creatures. As I discussed in the last chapter, make sure that you immediately pursue the employee who breaches the contract. You do not want to give the next employee who leaves the impression that you are not going to enforce the contract.

Confidentiality

In this paragraph all the members of the company are agreeing to keep the corporate transactions confidential. There would also have to be a paragraph stating what would happen if a member breaches the confidentiality clause.

Confidentiality: All MEMBERS who have signed below, hereby agree and consent not to discuss, disclose, advertise, or in any way make public, or discuss with any non-member any of the details, circumstances, events, facts, issues, or plans involving the company.

Governing Law/Venue: This lease shall be governed by the State of Florida and the venue shall be only in Palm Beach County, Florida.

It is also important to establish in a contract whose law will govern and where the venue will be when the contract needs to be interpreted.

Venue means, where the lawsuit will be brought. In the example above the lawsuit can only be brought in Palm Beach County, Florida. If that's where you live it is great for you because you will be on your home turf in case of a dispute. Governing law tells the judge where to look in order to interpret the contract. For example, if you have a non-compete clause in a contract you would want Florida law to govern. So, with the above contract clause, even if you go to court in Texas, the judge will be forced to use Florida law. You and the party you are contracting with can use whatever location you wish as the venue, as long as you include it in the contract, as shown in the above example.

Put all these clauses together and you have the starting point for a contract, from one party's point of view of course. Remember that the other side does not want the same provisions. In fact, they want the exact opposite. The key goes back to the beginning of the book. The side that has the most power will get the provisions they want in the contact. Also, be aware that this just scratches the surface of contracts. There are hundreds of other clauses and many different ways to word each paragraph. Discussing all of those items is far beyond the scope of a book this size, in fact, how you word each paragraph of the contract will change depending on each situation. Change one small fact and the entire texture of the contract can be different.

Some final advice; carefully number your contract so any person can trace the contract drafts and exhibits. For example, I may label a contract G0093-C. The "G" stands for my initial, which tells me I wrote the contract. The 93 is a unique number which refers to the contract. This number will be the reference for all internal and external correspondence concerning the document. The C means that there were three drafts of this document. I can look at drafts A and B and see the changes that were made. Changes are easily identified. Additions are underlined and items removed are struck through. In the next draft we will do the same thing with all new additions or removals. This is important. Anyone can pick up the file and trace the development of this contact.

Also, a word about the use of the term "reasonable". "Reasonable" is a very vague term. What is a "reasonable price"? Using the word "reasonable" is like leaving a blank in your contract that will need to be filled in. Usually the person who fills in that blank is a judge. By clearly defining what you want instead of using the term "reasonable", you avoid a dispute, which may require going to court to resolve it.

In conclusion, let me tell you that there is no substitute for a good lawyer. He or she is worth his/her weight in gold. Run any contract by an expert and ask for his/her help. It may take some money, time and trouble, but in the long run it will be well worth it.